BUTTERWORTHS
ANNOTATED LEGISLATION
SERVICE

STATUTES SUPPLEMENT No. 225

THE CONTROL OF POLLUTION ACT 1974

By

J. F. GARNER, LL.D(Lond.)

Solicitor, Professor of Public Law,
University of Nottingham

LONDON
BUTTERWORTHS
1975

ENGLAND: BUTTERWORTH & CO. (PUBLISHERS) LTD.
LONDON: 88 KINGSWAY, WC2B 6AB
AUSTRALIA: BUTTERWORTHS PTY. LTD.
SYDNEY: 586 PACIFIC HIGHWAY, CHATSWOOD, NSW 2067
MELBOURNE: 343 LITTLE COLLINS STREET, 3000
BRISBANE: 240 QUEEN STREET, 4000
CANADA: BUTTERWORTH & CO. (CANADA) LTD.
TORONTO: 2265 MIDLAND AVENUE, SCARBOROUGH, M1P 4S1
NEW ZEALAND: BUTTERWORTHS OF NEW ZEALAND LTD.
WELLINGTON: 26-28 WARING TAYLOR STREET, 1
SOUTH AFRICA: BUTTERWORTH & CO. (SOUTH AFRICA) (PTY.) LTD.
DURBAN: 152-154 GALE STREET

ISBN 0 406 54738 6

Printed in Great Britain by
Billing & Sons Limited
Guildford and London

PREFACE

The Control of Pollution Act 1974 can be regarded as a "breakthrough" in environmental legislation, or it may be thought of as a development of the public health and related legislation of the nineteenth and early twentieth centuries. Whether one takes the forward or the backward view there is no doubt but that it is an important and elaborate measure of great significance for lawyers in local government and private practice, and for those advising landowners and amenity societies. Its full effect will depend on the manner and extent of its implementation; it is hoped that the present volume will serve to assist practitioners and others readily to find their way round the complicated provisions, and to make the maximum use of this new machinery provided for the fight against the pollution of our environment in its many forms.

The book follows a standard pattern of a general introduction followed by the *ipsissima verba* of the Act. Each of the four substantive Parts is introduced by general comments, and the notes to the sections, besides giving cross references to definitions, include remarks about relevant case law and other statutes. The law is intended to be stated as at 30th November 1974.

December 1974 J. F. G.

CONTENTS

TABLE OF STATUTES

References in this Table to "Statutes" are to Halsbury's Statutes of England (Third Edition) showing the volume and page at which the annotated text of the Act will be found. Paragraph numbers printed in bold type indicate where The Control of Pollution Act 1974 is set out.

LIST OF CASES

INTRODUCTION

[**1**] The Control of Pollution Act 1974, which received Royal Assent on 31st July 1974, commenced life under the former Conservative Government as the Protection of the Environment Bill. After it had completed its life in the House of Lords under that guise it was taken over by the Socialist Government that came to power in March 1974 and was given its present title. Many of the amendments made to the first Bill in the Lords were incorporated in the print of the second Bill. The final title is a more apt description of the Act's objectives than was the original one, as the Act deals only with four main topics, namely, the control of the deposit and disposal of waste on land (Part I); the prevention of water pollution (Part II), including controls over underground water; the control of pollution by noise (Part III); and the control of pollution of the atmosphere (Part IV), which is concerned principally with motor vehicle exhausts, and leaves the Clean Air Acts 1956 and 1968 on the statute book. Because mainly of the new title, attempts by some of the members of the House of Lords in the early stages of the life of the first Bill, to introduce into the law a "general standard" for environmental protection, was abandoned. This notion of a general standard, which would have had the effect of requiring all government agencies to have regard to any potential harm to the environment as a consequence of the undertaking of any government or major private projects (such as the Channel Tunnel, or the establishment of a new oil refinery), was inspired by the National Environment Protection Act of the United States, which requires the formulation of an "environmental impact statement" before any major federal government project is undertaken. American experience has demonstrated the value of such a device, but some lawyers are of the opinion that if it were to be introduced in this country it would need to be reinforced by some form of judicial control and probably also a Protection Agency; s. 11 of the Countryside Act 1968, for example, does not seem to have made any considerable impact on governmental activity as it merely imposes an unenforceable duty to have regard to preservation of the countryside.

[**2**] Be that as it may, the present Act is a great step forward in conservation legislation. Part I not only tidies up a number of gaps in the law of refuse collection, paying due regard to local government reorganisation, but it also substitutes a licensing system for the deposit of controlled waste, for the somewhat unsatisfactory notification system of the Deposit of Poisonous Waste Act 1972 (repealed by Sch. 4). It is perhaps a trifle unfortunate that more positive requirements for the re-cycling of appropriate items of refuse have not been imposed on disposal and collection authorities,[1] but at least *powers* to

[1] Collection is the responsibility of the district councils in England while disposal is the responsibility of the county councils; in Wales both functions are the concern of the district councils: Local Government Act 1972.

re-cycle waste, and to purchase waste for the purpose, are conferred by s. 20, and s. 21 gives powers to produce heat and electricity from waste; there is also a requirement to the effect that thought must be given to this subject in the preparation of the waste disposal plans that are required under s. 2.

[3] Part II replaces almost all the provisions of the Rivers (Prevention of Pollution) Act 1951 and 1961, the whole of the Clean Rivers (Estuaries and Tidal Waters) Act 1960 and some sections of the Water Resources Act 1963. The method followed here is to strengthen existing law rather than to provide new methods of control. Thus, the defences available to persons causing pollution are restricted, and the controls now apply to virtually all inland (including some underground) and coastal waters. The existing system of controls over discharge of trade effluent into public sewers (under the Public Health (Drainage of Trade Premises) Act 1937, as amended) is retained, but is fully extended for the first time to pre-1937 discharges. Charges can therefore be made in future for pre- and post-1937 discharges of trade effluent to sewers, and also in respect of discharges to rivers and streams. This is clearly a step forward in the public interest, but it is to be hoped that water authorities generally will encourage industrialists to remove noxious elements at source before discharge; in some cases they may even be able to re-use minerals so extracted.

[4] Part III contains perhaps the most revolutionary provisions of the Act. The Noise Abatement Act 1960 is repealed but is replaced by similar provisions in ss. 58 and 62. More importantly, however, there are provisions whereby a district local authority may declare a "noise abatement zone" for an area within their district—a device clearly patterned on the smoke control areas of the Clean Air Acts. Even the procedure that must be followed in the process of making a noise abatement zone, prescribed in Sch. 1, resembles that applicable to the declaration of a smoke control area under the 1956 Act. The Act does not require an impossibility, by outlawing *all* noise within an abatement zone, but enables the authority to take action to prevent noise from specified premises of an intensity greater than the level prevailing at the time the zone was declared; in certain circumstances they can also require those noise levels to be reduced. The levels will be set presumably by reference to decibel limits, and enforcement officials would thus be relieved of the difficult task of deciding what is a reasonable or tolerable noise level, but as has been demonstrated by American exper ence, specified levels tend to become a minimum. The noise control provisions will apply to statutory undertakers (including, for example, British Railways), unlike the (repealed) Noise Abatement Act 1960, as they do to private companies, but the defence of "best practicable means" is given a special meaning in its application to statutory undertakers (see s. 65 (4)). Special powers exist to control noise levels on construction sites, but the problem of noise from aircraft is not dealt with, and s. 40 of the Civil Aviation Act 1949, providing a defence to common law proceedings in nuisance, is not affected by the Act. See also s. 1 (1) (*g*) of the Hovercraft Act 1968, as amended by Sch. 3 of this Act, under which an Order in Council may be made providing that proceedings may not be taken under this Act in respect of noise or vibration caused by a hovercraft. Until such an order is made, hovercraft are subject to the Act, being "vessels" by virtue of s. 105 (1).

[5] Part IV comes as somewhat of an anti-climax after reading the earlier

Parts, mainly of course because the Clean Air Acts of 1956 and 1968 have been so successful in abating pollution from smoke,[2] which was the principal cause of the great London "smog" of 1952.[3] The present Act is primarily concerned in dealing with air pollution caused by emissions from motor vehicles—the most serious form of atmospheric pollution virtually untouched by existing legislation. This it attempts to do by empowering the Secretary of State to make regulations as to the composition and content of fuel used in motor vehicles (s. 75), and also as to the sulphur content of oil fuel (s. 76). Presumably these regulations when made will effectively control the emission of lead into the atmosphere, a subject that has been much in the public awareness in recent months. It was perhaps unnecessary to provide in the Act for the compulsory introduction into vehicle design of mechanical devices to prevent noxious emissions from exhausts and crankcases of a pattern adopted in several of the American States, because such provisions could be (but have not yet been) introduced in Control and Use Regulations made under the Road Traffic Acts.[4]

[6] Part IV also includes clauses enabling a district local authority to undertake investigation and research into air pollution problems, and to publish information thereon (s. 79). They may require information to be provided as to the emission of air pollutants from specified premises. This Part does not deal with the alkali controls in any detail, although some of the procedural sections of the Act of 1906 have been repealed. For the present the powers of the Alkali Inspectorate are not altered, but these will be affected by the Health and Safety at Work etc. Act 1974.

[7] Part V, containing the inevitable supplementary provisions and Part VI, Miscellaneous and General, do not call for any specific comment here, except to point out that s. 99, incorporating Sch. 2, provides for substantial increases in penalties for pre-existing pollution offences.[5]

[8] *General Comments:* The Act applies to Scotland (with the usual necessary modifications)[6] but except for four sections[7] it does not apply to Northern Ireland.

[9] The common statutory defence to the effect that a person charged with a pollution offence had used the "best practicable means"[8] to avoid pollution,

---

[2] "Smoke", properly used to signify a visible vapour, is the principal concern of the Acts of 1956 and 1968, although there are also provisions designed to arrest the emission of grit and dust. The emission of noxious or polluting gases and fumes from industrial processes is controlled under the supervision of the centralised Alkali Inspectorate, under the Alkali, etc., Works Regulation Act 1906. Smoke control under the 1956–1968 Acts is, however, the concern of the district council.

[3] See the "Beaver" Report of 1954 (Cmd. 9322), which was the inspiration of the Clean Air Act 1956.

[4] But see the Motor Vehicles (Construction and Use) Regulations 1973, arts. 30–34 (S.I. 1973 No. 24). As to excessive noise, see arts. 29, 106, 107, 108.

[5] Contained in the Alkali, etc. Works Regulations Act 1906, the Public Health Act 1936, the Public Health (Drainage of Trade Premises) Act 1937, the Water Act 1945, the Rivers (Prevention of Pollution) Act 1951 and 1961, the Clean Air Acts 1956 and 1968 and the Radioactive Substances Act 1960.

[6] Contained in s. 96.

[7] Sections 75, 77, 100 and 101: see s. 109 (3).

[8] The expression "best practicable means" does not seem to have been defined in any leading cases, but as to "practicable measures", as used in the Factories Acts, see *Adsett* v. *K. and L. Steelfounders and Engineers, Ltd.*, [1953] 1 All E.R. 97, n. and *Gregson* v. *Hick Hargreaves & Co., Ltd.*, [1955] 3 All E.R. 507. For the purposes of the Clean Air Act 1956, "practicable means" includes the provision and maintenance of plant and the proper use thereof (Act of 1956, s. 34 (1)).

does not in terms appear in the water pollution prevention provisions (but see the special defences of s. 31 (2)). For the purposes of noise control, the expression has now been given a statutory definition (see s. 72), but this also does not apply to air pollution, and the defence in its unqualified form is still available in proceedings taken under the Alkali Act and in statutory nuisance proceedings under the Public Health Act 1936. It should be noted that the Act does not in general apply to Crown premises, except in so far as an interest in Crown land does not belong to Her Majesty and is not a "Crown interest" or a "Duchy interest"[9] (s. 105 (3)). Property belonging to a public corporation, other than one of the national health service corporations, will, however, be subject to the Act.[10]

[10] The Act is not a comprehensive code of environmental law. Some of its objectives, especially in the noise prevention field, could be achieved by a careful use of the machinery of town and country planning legislation (see Department of the Environment Circular 10/73). The abatement of noise within offices, factories and other places of work is barely dealt with (except under s. 68 and in relation to construction sites) by the present Act, but this could be achieved by regulations under the Factories Act 1961, and the Offices, Shops and Railway Premises Act 1963, as modified by the Health and Safety at Work etc. Act 1974. Except for a single section dealing with the treatment or disposal of waste or other matter (s. 101), the Act does not deal with pollution of the atmosphere by radioactive materials. Water pollution by such substances or the deposit of radioactive matter on land could presumably be dealt with by regulations under Parts I and II respectively, but alternative powers already exist under the Radioactive Substances Act 1960.

[11] Whereas the controls over water pollution contained in Part II apply to coastal waters (see definition of "controlled waters" in s. 56 (1)), the Act does not generally apply to marine waters outside the three-mile territorial limit;[11] such pollution is in some measure controlled by the Oil in Navigable Waters Acts 1955–1971 and the Prevention of Oil Pollution Act 1971.

[12] A problem of considerable topical interest is that of the disclosure of information. Section 94 prohibits under penalty the disclosure of any information relating to a trade secret obtained by virtue of the Act, and s. 12 of the Rivers (Prevention of Pollution) Act 1961, which is left unrepealed (see Sch. 4) is much to the same effect. Special provision is also made to a like effect in relation to information about air pollution (s. 79 (5)). However, there are a number of exceptions to this principle provided for in the Act, and they may be summarised as follows:

(*a*) if the disclosure was made in performance of a duty by the person disclosing the secret, or if it was made pursuant to a written consent;

(*b*) if the information was of a kind prescribed in regulations made under s. 94 by the Secretary of State;

---

[9] As defined in s. 266 of the Town and Country Planning Act 1971. As to Part IV, see s. 77 (2) and s. 80 (6).

[10] See *Tamlin* v. *Hannaford*, [1950] 1 K.B. 18; [1949] 2 All E.R. 527 and contrast *Nottingham Area No. 1 Hospital Management Committee* v. *Owen*, [1958] 1 Q.B. 50; [1957] 3 All E.R. 358.

[11] Except in relation to the discharge of sewage by means of a pipe from the land; see s. 32.

(*c*) if the information related to the problem of air pollution and was published in accordance with s. 79 (1) (*b*);

(*d*) if the information related to consents or samples of effluent and it is required to be recorded in a register maintained pursuant to regulations made by the Secretary of State under s. 41, and the particular information has not been exempted from this requirement by a certificate under s. 42.

[Cases (*a*), (*b*) and (*c*) above are provided for in s. 94 itself; case (*d*) depends on ss. 41 and 42.]

[13] Enforcement and administration of Parts I and III of the Act will be the concern of local authorities (the district councils, except for the disposal of waste in England, which is the responsibility of county councils). Enforcement of any regulations made by the Secretary of State concerning the composition, etc., of motor fuel will be the concern of weights and measures authorities (the county councils, and designated district councils in Wales: Local Government Act 1972) and the enforcement of water pollution provisions of Part II are the concern of water authorities,[12] who, since the coming into operation of the Water Act 1973 on 1st April 1974, have taken over from local authorities all responsibility for sewerage and sewage disposal, and also for the collection, protection and distribution of water supplies. Legal proceedings for offences under the Act (in particular under Part III) may be instituted by local authorities under s. 222 of the Local Government Act 1972.

[14] The system of appeals against decisions of authorities is complicated; sometimes an appeal lies to the Secretary of State, from whom no further appeal is expressly provided for, except that in one case he may be required to state a case (s. 39 (8)). In any case he may order the convening of a local inquiry (s. 96); sometimes he may be required to do so (e.g. s. 35 (2)). In other cases (in particular in several instances under Part III) an appeal lies in the first instance to the local magistrates; in those cases an appeal will always lie from the magistrates to the Crown Court under s. 85, if not under any other enactment (as to appeals under Part III see also s. 65). If there is a right of appeal to a magistrates court from a decision of a local water authority, this must be notified to the person concerned with the decision (s. 87 (4)).

[15] In yet other cases matters of dispute between administrative authorities may fall to be determined by the Secretary of State (see, for example, s. 11 (5)); no provision is made for the procedure to be followed in such cases, nor is there any right of further appeal on a point of law to the courts. There are also a few instances where disputes fall to be determined by arbitration, in which event the Arbitration Act 1950 will apply (see s. 31 (1) thereof). It is a further outstanding feature of this Act that almost every section gives power to the Secretary of State for the Environment (herein called "the Secretary of State") to make regulations either generally, or "prescribing" particular matters.[13]

---

[12] In most of Wales, the Welsh National Water Development Authority (Water Act 1973, s. 2). In addition there are nine regional water authorities covering England and the remainder of Wales (*ibid.*, Schedule 1).

[13] Orders and regulations must be made by way of statutory instruments which (subject to a few exceptions) will be subject to the negative resolution procedure in Parliament: see s. 104. Byelaws made by water authorities must comply with the procedure of the Water Act 1973, as amended by Sch. 3 of this Act.

Until these Regulations have been made, it is difficult in many contexts to visualise precisely how the statute will operate in practice.

[**16**] The Act is to come into force on such day or days as the Secretary of State may by order or orders appoint (s. 109 (2)). At the date of going to press the following sections had been brought into force by The Control of Pollution Act 1974 (Commencement No. 1) Order 1974 (S.I. 1974 No. 2039): ss. 43, 44, 95, 104, 105, 107, 108 (1) (so far as it applies to para. 27 of Sch. 3) and 109.

THE CONTROL OF POLLUTION ACT 1974

(1974 c. 40)

ARRANGEMENT OF SECTIONS

PART I

WASTE ON LAND

Waste disposal arrangements

PART I

WASTE ON LAND

INTRODUCTION TO PART I

[**17**] This Part is concerned with the collection and disposal of "waste" of various kinds. The Act is principally concerned with controlled waste (i.e. household, industrial and commercial waste), but the Secretary of State may make regulations applying prescribed provisions of Part I to other specified kinds of waste, such as farm waste or mine or quarry waste, within a prescribed area (see s. 18); all these specialised expressions, including "waste" itself, are defined in s. 30.

[**18**] Disposal authorities (district councils in Wales, county councils and the G.L.C. in England: s. 30) have a duty to make adequate arrangements for disposing of controlled waste (s. 1) and to carry out investigations and as a consequence, prepare comprehensive "waste disposal plans", after consultation with other authorities, and within such time as may be directed by the Secretary of State (s. 2). The general prohibition on the deposit of waste that might cause an environmental hazard, and the notification system, contained in the Deposit of Poisonous Waste Act 1972, has been repealed (Sch. 4), but these provisions are replaced by a licensing system (ss. 3–11). By virtue of s. 3, controlled waste may be deposited

only on land occupied by a licence holder issued under s. 5 (and see s. 16) although s. 4 includes transitional provisions authorising existing arrangements. Licences are to be issued by disposal authorities, and planning permission must first have been obtained (unless such is not required under planning legislation in respect of the land in question). A licence may be issued subject to conditions authorised under regulations made by the Secretary of State and also those expressly listed in s. 6 (2), and a register of licences must be maintained by the disposal authority (s. 6 (4)). Provision is made for the variation of conditions and revocation of licences (s. 7), for the transfer of licences (s. 8) and for the supervision by the disposal authority of activities authorised by a licence (s. 9). Appeals against a refusal of a disposal licence or conditions contained therein, or against a revocation of a licence, lie to the Secretary of State (s. 10). There is no provision entitling an appellant to a hearing on such an appeal, but if he saw fit the Secretary of State could order the holding of a local inquiry into an appeal, under s. 96. There is also no provision for a right of appeal on a point of law to the High Court from a decision of the Secretary of State, but in a proper case no doubt a declaration, or possibly a *certiorari* (see *R.* v. *Hillingdon London Borough Council Ex parte Royco Homes, Ltd.* [1974] 2 All E.R. 643) would lie. Section 11 makes special provision for land occupied by disposal authorities, requiring them in effect to observe precautions similar to those imposed on licence holders.

[**19**] Sections 12–17, concerned principally with the duties of collection authorities (district councils, London Borough councils, the Common Council of the City and the two Temples: s. 30 (1), replace the relevant provisions (ss. 72–77) of the Public Health Act 1936 as amended by the Local Government Act 1972. There is a general duty to collect controlled waste (subject to certain limited exceptions) imposed by s. 12 (it being no longer necessary for the local authority to give an undertaking to do so, as under s. 72 of the Public Health Act 1936) and it is provided that no charge may be made for the collection of household waste; there is also provision for the emptying of privies and cesspools. Section 13 is concerned with the use and provision of "dustbins", and it is made clear that a dustbin includes a holder for a waste receptacle (sack-holders): s. 13 (8). Section 14 is concerned with the disposal of waste so collected. Section 16 empowers a disposal authority to require the occupier of land on which controlled waste has been deposited otherwise than in accordance with a disposal licence, to remove the waste. Finally, by s. 17 the Secretary of State may make regulations for the disposal of waste of a particularly dangerous kind, or of a kind that it is difficult to dispose of. Section 19 empowers a disposal authority to collect information about waste disposal, and ss. 91–94 will not apply to any such information (see Part V).

[**20**] Sections 20 and 21 are concerned with the reclamation of waste. Section 20 empowers disposal authorities to arrange for the re-cycling of waste and the reclamation of substances from waste, and also to buy and sell waste. Section 21 empowers disposal authorities to use waste for the production of heat and electricity and to sell heat or electricity so produced, but in the case of electricity they must first consult with the Central Electricity Generating Board and the local Electricity Board unless they are using the electricity solely at the waste disposal installation.

[**21**] Section 22 is concerned with the duties of highway and local authorities to arrange for the cleaning of highways and s. 23 contains elaborate provisions enabling a highway authority or local authority to prohibit the parking of vehicles in a relevant area, so as to facilitate street cleaning in that area. Section 24 requires all local authorities to consider from time to time what steps ought to be taken for the abatement of litter. (The Litter Acts of 1958 and 1969 are left unrepealed.) Section 25 deals with the disposal of waste underground by the National Coal Board and their licensees. Section 26 is perhaps somewhat out of place, in that it provides for

the laying of outfall pipes for sewage disposal works in streets, by an extension of Part 3 of the Water Act 1945. Section 27 is of more general application, making "totting" or the sorting over or disturbing of the contents of a refuse tip or a dustbin an offence. Section 28 deals with the laying of pipes for waste disposal. Section 29 gives power to the Secretary of State to make regulations modifying the provisions of Part I or Part II so as to avoid any duplication of control imposed by the two Parts respectively, and s. 30 is the interpretation section for Part I.

[Royal Assent was given on 31st July 1974.]

Waste disposal arrangements

1. Arrangements for disposing of controlled waste

It shall be the duty of each disposal authority to ensure that the arrangements made by the authority and other persons for the disposal of waste are adequate for the purpose of disposing of all controlled waste which becomes situated in its area after this section comes into force and all controlled waste which is likely to become so situated. [22]

DEFINITIONS

Controlled waste:	s. 30 (1)
Disposal authority:	s. 30 (1)
Waste:	s. 30 (1) and see s. 30 (3).

GENERAL NOTE

This duty may be enforced by means of a default order made by the Secretary of State under s. 97. The section will come into force when an order is made by the Secretary of State under s. 109 (2).

Waste disposal plans

2. Preparation and revision of waste disposal plans

(1) It shall be the duty of each disposal authority—

(*a*) to carry out an investigation with a view to deciding what arrangements are needed for the purpose of disposing of controlled waste which is situated in its area and of controlled waste which is likely to be so situated;

(*b*) to decide what arrangements are in the opinion of the authority needed for that purpose;

(*c*) to prepare a statement of the arrangements made and proposed to be made by the authority and other persons for disposing of such waste during a period specified in the statement (hereafter in this section referred to as "the plan");

(*d*) to carry out from time to time further investigations with a view to deciding what changes in the plan are needed for the purpose aforesaid; and

(*e*) to make any modification of the plan which the authority thinks appropriate in consequence of any further investigation in pursuance of the preceding paragraph;

and in considering any arrangements or modification for the purposes of paragraph (*c*) or (*e*) of this subsection it shall be the duty of the authority to have regard to the effect which the arrangements or modification would be likely to have on the amenities of any relevant locality and to the likely cost to the authority of the arrangements or modification.

(2) It shall be the duty of a disposal authority to include in the plan information as to—

(*a*) the kinds and quantities of controlled waste which the authority expects will be situated in its area during the period specified in the plan;

(*b*) the kinds and quantities of controlled waste which the authority expects to be brought for disposal into or taken for disposal out of the authority's area during that period;

(*c*) the kinds and quantities of controlled waste which the authority expects to dispose of itself during that period;

(*d*) the kinds and quantities of controlled waste which the authority expects to be disposed of in its area during that period by persons other than the authority;

(*e*) the methods by which in the opinion of the authority controlled waste in its area should be disposed of, either by reclaiming substances from it or otherwise, during that period and the priorities which in its opinion should be accorded during that period to the provision of different methods of disposal;

(*f*) the sites and equipment which the authority and other persons are providing and during that period proposes itself to provide and expects other persons to provide for disposing of controlled waste; and

(*g*) the estimated costs of the methods of disposal mentioned in the plan;

but provision may be made by regulations for modifying paragraphs (*a*) to (*g*) of this subsection and for requiring a disposal authority to take prescribed factors into account in preparing the plan and any modification of it.

(3) It shall be the duty of a disposal authority—

(*a*) in preparing the plan and any modification of it, to consult—

(i) any water authority any part of whose area is included in the area of the disposal authority, except where the plan or modification is prepared by an islands council, and

(ii) in a case where the plan or modification is prepared by an English disposal authority, the collection authorities whose areas are included in the area of the disposal authority, and

(iii) (*applies to Scotland*), and

(iv) in a case where the plan or modification is prepared by a disposal authority of which the area is in Wales, the county council whose area includes that of the authority, and

(v) in a case where provisions of the plan or modification relate to the taking of waste for disposal into the area of another disposal authority, that other authority, and

(vi) in any case, such persons as the disposal authority considers it appropriate to consult from among persons who in the opinion of the authority are or are likely to be, or are representative of persons who are or are likely to be, engaged by way of trade or business in the disposal or controlled waste situated in the area of the authority, and such other persons as are prescribed; and

(*b*) before finally determining the content of the plan or modification (excluding a modification which in the opinion of the authority is such that no person will be prejudiced if the following provisions of this paragraph are disregarded with respect to it), to take such steps as in the opinion of the authority will—

(i) give adequate publicity in its area to the plan or modification, and

(ii) provide members of the public with opportunities of making representations to the authority about it,

and to consider any representations made in pursuance of sub-paragraph (ii) of this paragraph and make any change in the plan or modification which the authority considers appropriate in consequence of the representations.

(4) Without prejudice to the generality of the duty imposed on disposal authorities by the preceding subsection, it shall be the duty of a disposal authority, in preparing the plan and any modification of it (excluding a modification which the authority considers irrelevant for the purposes of this subsection), to consider, in consultation with such persons as the authority considers appropriate and as agree to participate in the consultations and, in the case of an English disposal authority, in consultation with the collection authorities whose areas are included in the area of the disposal authority,—

(*a*) what arrangements can reasonably be expected to be made for the purpose of reclaiming substances from controlled waste which is situated in the area of the disposal authority; and

(*b*) what provisions should be included in the plan for that purpose.

(5) A disposal authority shall not finally determine the content of the plan or a modification of it in a case falling within paragraph (*a*) (v) of subsection (3) of this section except with the consent of the other disposal authority, or if the other authority withholds its consent, with the consent of the Secretary of State.

(6) When a disposal authority has finally determined the content of the plan or a modification of it in accordance with the preceding provisions of this section it shall be the duty of the authority—

(*a*) to take such steps as in the opinion of the authority will give adequate publicity in its area to the plan or modification; and

(*b*) to send to the Secretary of State a copy of the plan or, as the case may be, particulars of the modification.

(7) The Secretary of State may give to any authority a direction as to the time by which the authority is to perform any duty specified in the direction which is imposed on the authority by the preceding provisions of this section; and it shall be the duty of the authority to comply with the direction. [**23**]

DEFINITIONS

Collection authority:	s. 30 (1)
Controlled waste:	s. 30(1)
Disposal authority:	s. 30 (1)
English disposal authority:	s. 30 (1)
The "plan":	sub-s. (1) (*c*)
Regulations; made by the Secretary of State under	
Waste:	s. 30 (1) and s. 104; s. 105(1) (3).
Water authorities:	Water Act 1973, s. 2.

GENERAL NOTE

Although a waste disposal plan does not have to be confirmed by the Secretary of State, there is a duty to send him a copy (sub-s. (6)), and he may give directions as to the time within which the authority must perform any duty imposed under this section (see sub-s. (9)). A dispute between two authorities may also have to be determined by the Secretary of State: sub-s. (5). Failure to prepare a plan could be made the subject of a default order under s. 97. The requirements of sub-s. (2) may be modified by regulations made by the Secretary of State. A local authority has a general power to obtain information required for the purposes of preparing their plan (or otherwise) under s. 93.

In preparing their waste disposal plan, local authorities should also be mindful of their duty to provide public tips under s. 18 of the Civic Amenities Act 1967 (as amended by sch. 3). If refuse tips are left unfenced in conditions where children may be expected to trespass, the local authority may be liable in tort for injuries suffered by such a child, unless the authority can be shown to have acted reasonably as a "human occupier"; see *Penny* v. *Northampton Borough Council*, (1974), 118 Sol. Jo. 628, applying the principle in *British Railways Board* v. *Hemington*, (118 Sol. Jo. 628 [1972] A.C. 877; [1972] 1 All E.R. 749. As to the powers of local authorities to re-use waste, see ss. 20 and 21.

SUB-S. (2)

The plan does not necessarily have to provide for the disposal of "special" waste (see s. 17).

SUB-S. (3)

As to the duty to consult, see *Rollo* v. *Minister of Town and Country Planning*, [1948] 1 All E.R. 13. It is interesting that para. (*a*) (vi) in effect requires consultation with persons in the disposal industry.

SUB-S. (4)

As to this further limited duty to consult, see *Agricultural, Horticultural and Forestry Industry Training Board* v. *Aylesbury Mushrooms, Ltd.* [1972] 1 All E.R. 280. The authority must, it seems, consult with *some* persons, but the choice of persons to be consulted is at the discretion of the disposal authority. In addition an English disposal authority *must* consult with appropriate collection authorities.

Licensing of disposal of controlled waste

3. Prohibition of unlicensed disposal of waste

(1) Except in prescribed cases, a person shall not—

(*a*) deposit controlled waste on any land or cause or knowingly permit controlled waste to be deposited on any land; or

(*b*) use any plant or equipment, or cause or knowingly permit any plant or equipment to be used, for the purpose of disposing of controlled waste or of dealing in a prescribed manner with controlled waste,

unless the land on which the waste is deposited or, as the case may be, which forms the site of the plant or equipment is occupied by the holder of a licence issued in pursuance of section 5 of this Act (in this Part of this Act referred to as a "disposal licence") which authorises the deposit or use in question and the deposit or use is in accordance with the conditions, if any, specified in the licence.

(2) Except in a case falling within the following subsection, a person who contravenes any of the provisions of the preceding subsection shall, subject to subsection (4) of this section, be guilty of an offence and liable on summary conviction to a fine of an amount not exceeding £400 or on conviction on indictment to imprisonment for a term not exceeding two years or a fine or both.

(3) A person who contravenes paragraph (*a*) of subsection (1) of this section in a case where—

(*a*) the waste in question is of a kind which is poisonous, noxious or polluting; and

(*b*) its presence on the land is likely to give rise to an environmental hazard; and

(*c*) it is deposited on the land in such circumstances or for such a period that whoever deposited it there may reasonably be assumed to have abandoned it there or to have brought it there for the purpose of its being disposed of (whether by himself or others) as waste,

shall, subject to the following subsection, be guilty of an offence and liable on summary conviction to imprisonment for a term not exceeding six months or a fine not exceeding £400 or both or on conviction on indictment to imprisonment for a term not exceeding five years or a fine or both.

(4) It shall be a defence for a person charged with an offence under this section to prove—

(*a*) that he—

(i) took care to inform himself, from persons who were in a position to provide the information, as to whether the deposit or use to which the charge relates would be in contravention of subsection (1) of this section, and

(ii) did not know and had no reason to suppose that the information given to him was false or misleading and that the deposit or use might be in contravention of that subsection; or

(*b*) that he acted under instructions from his employer and neither knew nor had reason to suppose that the deposit or use was in contravention of the said subsection (1); or

(*c*) in the case of an offence of making, causing or permitting a deposit or use otherwise than in accordance with conditions specified in a disposal licence, that he took all such steps as were reasonably open to him to ensure that the conditions were complied with; or

(*d*) that the acts specified in the charge were done in an emergency in order to avoid danger to the public and that, as soon as reasonably practicable after they were done, particulars of them were furnished to the disposal authority in whose area the acts were done. [**24**]

DEFINITIONS

Controlled waste:	s. 30 (1)
Disposal authority:	s. 30 (1)
Disposal licence:	see sub-s. (1), proviso
Holder [of a licence]:	s. 8 (3)
Land:	includes water; see s. 4 (4)
Prescribed:	i.e., by regulations made by the Secretary of State: s. 105 (1)
Waste:	s. 30 (1), and see s. 30 (3)

GENERAL NOTE

This important section (which should be read with s. 4) introduces the system for the licensing of the deposit of controlled waste, which may be extended by the Secretary of State's regulations made under s. 18 to specified types of mine or quarry waste in prescribed areas. Unless a licence has been issued under s. 5 to the occupier of the land (an expression which may include water: see s. 4 (4)), it is an offence for controlled waste to be deposited on the land, or plant or equipment to be used for the purpose of disposing of any such waste. Regulations made by the Secretary of State may make exceptions for prescribed cases, and they may also provide that particular conditions may be disregarded (s. 6 (1)). If a disposal licence permits specified waste to be disposed of in a specified stream or other waters (in consultation with the water authority: s. 5 (4)), any disposal in accordance with the terms of such a licence will not constitute an offence against s. 26 (1).

As to conditions imposed in a disposal licence generally, see s. 6 (2). The procedure regulating applications for licences and their determination is contained in ss. 5 and 6. If an application for a licence is not dealt with within two months, it is to be deemed to have been rejected: s. 6 (5).

An appeal lies to the Secretary of State against an actual or deemed rejection of a licence, or against conditions imposed therein: s. 10 (1).

Subsections (1) does not apply to land occupied by the disposal authority: s. 11.

SUB-S (1)

"Cause or knowingly permit": see *Alphacell, Ltd.* v. *Woodward*, [1972] A.C. 824; [1972] 2 All E.R. 475, and s. 31 of this Act. For defences to an offence under this subsection, other than that provided by the existence of a disposal licence (but there must then be compliance with any conditions therein specified: see s. 5 (3)) see sub-s. (4) of this section. It should also be noted that the section does not apply to the disposal of household waste from a private dwelling within the curtilage: see s. 4 (2). Regulations may make other exceptions: see s. 4 (3).

SUB-S. 2

In a case falling within sub-s. (3) the maximum penalties are more stringent. The time limit within which proceedings for a summary offence under this sub-s. or under sub-s. (3) is one year: see s. 87 (3).

If a lorry driver deposits waste on land contrary to sub-s. (1) he will *prima facie* be liable under this sub-s. (2); if he is acting in the course of his employment and is not merely on a "frolic of his own" (so as, for example, to save himself time), his employer or firm may be liable. A corporate body will be liable if it can be established that responsibility for the offence can be ascribed to some person who is sufficiently senior in the company management to be "identifiable" with his company: see *Tesco Supermarkets, Ltd.* v. *Nattrass* [1972] A.C. 153; [1971] 2 All E.R. 127. If the lorry driver is acting under the clear instructions of a foreman or other supervisor, the foreman, etc., may be liable (s. 87 (2)), and the director, manager or other similar officer (or the members) of a body corporate may be liable under the present provisions in cases where the body corporate is primarily responsible (s. 87 (1)). The lorry driver himself may have a defence under sub-s. 4 (*a*) or (*b*) if he has (for example) asked a superior whether he may dump the waste on the land in question.

SUB-S. (3)

"Poisonous, noxious or polluting" is an expression that has been used in earlier legislation (see, in particular, the Rivers (Prevention of Pollution) Act 1951, s. 2) but it does not seem to have been interpreted by the courts. Presumably it is wide enough to include waste that is harmful to fauna or possibly to flora, even if it is harmless to human beings. Tin cans, etc., with sharp edges that might cut a person walking over the land (or broken glass in a pond) is perhaps neither poisonous nor polluting, but may be "noxious". As to what constitutes an "environmental hazard", see s. 4 (5). Sub-para. (*c*) seems to cover the case where there is a danger that the containers may be broken or may leak. If damage is caused as a consequence of any such deposit, the person responsible may be liable civilly to the person suffering such damage, but the defendant would then be entitled to plead the three factors listed in this subsection by way of a defence in such civil proceedings: see s. 88. As to time limits for proceedings, see note to sub-s. (2).

SUB-S. (4)

These defences may be important in circumstances such as the deposit of dangerous substances on roadside waste made necessary by an accident to a vehicle carrying the substances.

4. Provisions supplementary to s. 3

(1) Where activities for which a disposal licence is required apart from this subsection have been carried on on any land during the period of six months ending with the date when subsection (1) of the preceding section comes into force, nothing in that subsection shall apply to the carrying on of those activities on the land during the period of one year beginning with that date and, where at the end of that period an appeal is pending in pursuance of section 10 of this Act against a rejection of an application for a disposal licence in respect of those activities on the land or against a decision to issue such a licence which specifies conditions, until the appeal is determined.

(2) Nothing in subsection (1) of the preceding section applies to household waste from a private dwelling which is deposited, disposed of or dealt with within the curtilage of the dwelling by or with the permission of the occupier of the dwelling.

(3) It shall be the duty of the Secretary of State, in exercising the power conferred on him by subsection (1) of the preceding section to prescribe excepted cases, to have regard in particular to the expediency of excluding from the controls imposed by virtue of that subsection—

(*a*) any deposits which are small enough to be properly excluded from those controls or are of such a temporary nature that they may be so excluded;

(*b*) any uses of plant or equipment which are innocuous enough to be so excluded;

(*c*) cases for which adequate controls are provided by an enactment other than that subsection;

and without prejudice to the generality of section 104 (1) (*a*) of this Act the said power may be so exercised as to prescribe different excepted cases for different areas.

(4) References to land in the preceding section and this section include references to water which covers any land above low-water mark of ordinary spring tides and is not water in a stream within the meaning of Part II of this Act.

(5) For the purposes of subsection (3) of the preceding section—

(*a*) the presence of waste on land gives rise to an environmental hazard if the waste has been deposited in such a manner or in such a quantity (whether that quantity by itself or cumulatively with other deposits of the same or different substances) as to subject persons or animals to a material risk of death, injury or impairment of health or as to threaten the pollution (whether on the surface or underground) of any water supply; and

(*b*) the fact that waste is deposited in containers shall not of itself be taken to exclude any risk which might be expected to arise if the waste were not in containers.

(6) In the case of any deposit of waste, the degree of risk relevant for the purposes of the preceding subsection shall be assessed with particular regard—

(*a*) to the measures, if any, taken by the person depositing the waste, or by the owner or occupier of the land, or by others, for minimising the risk; and

(*b*) to the likelihood of the waste, or any container in which it is deposited, being tampered with by children or others. **[25]**

DEFINITIONS

Disposal licence:	s. 3 (1)
Household waste:	s. 30 (3)
Land:	see sub-s. (4)
Prescribe:	by regulations made by the Secretary of State, s. 105 (1)
Private dwelling:	s. 30 (1)
Stream:	s. 56 (1), applied by sub-s. (4)
Waste:	s. 30 (1), and see s. 30 (3)

GENERAL NOTE

Subsection (1) of this section is a transitional provision, enabling activities that would otherwise require to be licensed under this Part, to be exempt from the need to obtain a licence if they have been carried on for a period of six months before the appointed day when s. 3 came into force. The exemption will continue for a period of one year from that date, thereby allowing a person concerned that period within which to apply for a disposal licence. The other subsections complement the substantive provisions of s. 3.

SUB-S. (3)

The Secretary of State is under an express duty to consider excluding these matters from the operation of s. 3, but it would seem difficult for the duty to be enforced against him.

5. Licences to dispose of waste

(1) An application for a disposal licence in respect of any land in the area of a disposal authority must be made in writing to the authority and include such information as is prescribed.

(2) A disposal licence shall not be issued for a use of land, plant or equipment for which planning permission is required in pursuance of the Town and Country Planning Act 1971 or, in Scotland, the Town and Country Planning (Scotland) Act 1972 unless such permission is in force; but provision may be made by regulations for an application for a disposal licence to be considered while an application for any relevant planning permission is pending and for any proceedings connected with either application to be conducted concurrently with any proceedings connected with the other application.

(3) Where a disposal authority receives an application for a disposal licence

for a use of land, plant or equipment for which such planning permission as aforesaid is in force, it shall be the duty of the authority not to reject the application unless the authority is satisfied that its rejection is necessary for the purpose of preventing pollution of water or danger to public health.

(4) Where a disposal authority proposes to issue a disposal licence, it shall be the duty of the authority before it does so—

(*a*) to refer the proposal to the water authority and any collection authority of which the area includes any of the relevant land and to any other prescribed person; and

(*b*) to consider any representations about the proposal which, during the period of twenty-one days beginning with that on which the proposal is received by a body or person mentioned in paragraph (*a*) of this subsection or during such longer period as the disposal authority and that body or person agree in writing, the dispoasl authority receives from that body or person (including in particular any representations about the conditions which that body or person considers should be specified in the licence);

and if a water authority to which the proposal is referred requests the disposal authority not to issue the licence or disagrees with the disposal authority as to the conditions to be specified in the licence either of them may refer the matter to the Secretary of State and the licence shall not be issued except in accordance with his decision.

(5) [*Applies to Scotland only.*]

(6) A person who, in an application for a disposal licence, makes any statement which he knows to be false in a material particular or recklessly makes any statement which is false in a material particular shall be guilty of an offence and liable on summary conviction to a fine not exceeding £400 or on conviction on indictment to imprisonment for a term not exceeding two years or a fine or both.

[**26**]

DEFINITIONS

Collection authority:	s. 30 (1)
Disposal authority:	s. 30 (1)
Disposal licence:	s. 3 (1)
Land:	s. 6 (6) and s. 4 (4)
Prescribed:	by regulations made by the Secretary of State: s. 105 (1)
Regulations:	of the Secretary of State: s. 104 and 105 (1)
Relevant land:	s. 30 (1) and s. 4 (4)
Water authority:	Water Act 1973, s. 2

GENERAL NOTE

This section (with s. 6) is concerned with the procedure for the issue of disposal licences (required under s. 3), and in particular integrates the procedure with that for the issue of planning permissions under the Town and Country Planning Act 1971.

SUB-S. (1)

It seems that the actual application form is not to be prescribed, but the application must give all information that may be prescribed in the Secretary of State's regulations. Note that it should be made to the *disposal* authority, not the collection authority, although the disposal authority will have to consult the collection authority before determining the application: sub-s. (4).

SUB-S. (2)

Planning permission is not required for all activities involving the deposit of waste on land: see in particular Town and Country Planning Act 1971, s. 22 (3) (*b*) and the General Development Order 1973, Sch. 1, Class VIII, para. 2, Class XIII, para. 2, and Class XX. Planning permission is, however, always required for the opening of a new refuse tip. Both collection and disposal authorities will be planning authorities (Local Government Act 1972, Sch. 16), and therefore presumably the regulations to be made under this subsection will provide that applications for planning permission which are coupled with applications for a disposal licence under this Act, must be dealt with by the (county) disposal authorities.

SUB-S. (3)

The expressions "pollution of water" and "danger to public health" are not defined in the Act, but should be contrasted with the explanation of the expression "environmental hazard" in s. 4 (5).

SUB-S. (4)

Note the expressions "refer the proposals to", and "consider any representations"; it is not clear that they add much in practice to the more usual requirement for "consultation with" (see, for example, s. 2 (3)). Presumably a purported licence that has inadvertently been issued without observance of this mandatory procedure will be void *ab initio*: contrast the position as to notices and certificates under ss. 26 and 27 of the Town and Country Planning Act 1971.

SUB-S. (6)

As to offences by corporations, see s. 87.

6. Provisions supplementary to s. 5

(1) Provision may be made by regulations as to the conditions which are or are not to be specified in a disposal licence and as to the conditions specified in a disposal licence which shall be disregarded for the purposes of sections 3 (1) and 31 (2) (*a*) of this Act.

(2) Subject to regulations made in pursuance of the preceding subsection, a disposal licence may include such conditions as the disposal authority which issues it sees fit to specify in the licence; and without prejudice to the generality of the preceding provisions of this subsection, any such conditions may relate to—

(*a*) the duration of the licence;
(*b*) the supervision by the holder of the licence of activities to which the licence relates;
(*c*) the kinds and quantities of waste which may be dealt with in pursuance of the licence or which may be so dealt with during a specified period, the methods of dealing with them and the recording of information relating to them;
(*d*) the precautions to be taken on any land to which the licence relates;
(*e*) the steps to be taken with a view to facilitating compliance with any conditions of such planning permission as is mentioned in subsection (2) of the preceding section;
(*f*) the hours during which waste may be dealt with in pursuance of the licence; and

(*g*) the works to be carried out, in connection with the land, plant or equipment to which the licence relates, before the activities authorised by the licence are begun or while they are continuing;

and it is hereby declared that a condition may require the carrying out of works or the doing of any other thing which the authority considers appropriate in connection with the licence notwithstanding that the licence holder is not entitled as of right to carry out the works or do the thing.

(3) The holder of a disposal licence who without reasonable excuse contravenes a condition of the licence which in pursuance of regulations made by virtue of subsection (1) of this section is to be disregarded for the purposes mentioned in that subsection shall be guilty of an offence and liable on summary conviction to a fine not exceeding £400; but no proceedings for such an offence shall be brought in England and Wales except by or with the consent of the Director of Public Prosecutions or by the disposal authority which issued the licence.

(4) It shall be the duty of each disposal authority—

(*a*) to maintain a register containing prescribed particulars of all disposal licences issued by the authority which are for the time being in force; and

(*b*) to secure that the register is open to inspection at its principal office by members of the public free of charge at all reasonable hours; and

(*c*) to afford members of the public reasonable facilities for obtaining from the authority, on payment of reasonable charges, copies of entries in the register.

(5) If within the period of two months beginning with the date on which a disposal authority receives an application duly made to it for a disposal licence, or within such longer period as the authority and the applicant may at any time agree in writing, the authority has neither issued a licence in consequence of the application nor given notice to the applicant that the authority has rejected the application, the authority shall be deemed to have rejected the application.

(6) References to land in the preceding section and this section include such water as is mentioned in section 4 (4) of this Act. [**27**]

DEFINITIONS

Disposal authority:	s. 30 (1)
Disposal licence:	s. 3 (1)
Holder [of a licence]:	s. 8 (3)
Land:	sub-s. (6) and s. 4 (4)
Prescribed:	by regulations: s. 105 (1)
Regulations:	of the Secretary of State: s. 105 (1)

SUB-S. (4)

This register must include particulars of a resolution passed by a disposal authority under s. 11 (3) or (6) in respect of land occupied by them: s. 11 (10).

7. Variation of conditions and revocation of licences

(1) While a disposal licence issued by a disposal authority is in force, then—

(*a*) subject to any regulations in force by virtue of subsection (1) of the preceding section, the authority may—

(i) on its own initiative, serve a notice on the holder of the licence modifying the conditions specified in the licence to any extent which, in the opinion of the authority, is desirable and is unlikely to require unreasonable expenditure by the licence holder, and

(ii) on the application of the licence holder, serve a notice on him modifying the said conditions to the extent requested in the application;

and

(*b*) it shall be the duty of the authority to serve a notice on the licence holder modifying the conditions specified in the licence—

(i) subject to subsection (4) of this section, to the extent which in the opinion of the authority is required for the purpose mentioned in section 9 (1) (*a*) of this Act, and

(ii) to the extent required by any regulations in force as aforesaid.

(2) Subsection (4) or, in relation to Scotland, subsection (5) of section 5 of this Act shall with the necessary modifications apply to a proposal to serve a notice in pursuance of paragraph (*a*) or paragraph (*b*) (i) of the preceding subsection as it applies to a proposal to issue a disposal licence, except that—

(*a*) the disposal authority may postpone the reference in pursuance of the said subsection (4) or (5) so far as the authority considers that by reason of an emergency it is appropriate to do so; and

(*b*) the disposal authority may disregard any other authority for the purposes of the preceding provisions of this subsection in relation to a modification which, in the opinion of the disposal authority, will not affect the other authority.

(3) Section 5 (6) of this Act shall apply to an application in pursuance of subsection (1) (*a*) (ii) of this section as it applies to an application for a disposal licence.

(4) Where a disposal licence issued by a disposal authority is in force and it appears to the authority—

(*a*) that the continuation of activities to which the licence relates would cause pollution of water or danger to public health or would be so seriously detrimental to the amenities of the locality affected by the activities that the continuation of them ought not to be permitted; and

(*b*) that the pollution, danger or detriment cannot be avoided by modifying the conditions specified in the licence,

it shall be the duty of the authority by a notice served on the holder of the licence to revoke the licence.

(5) A notice served in pursuance of this section shall state the time at which the modification or revocation in question is to take effect. [**28**]

DEFINITIONS

Disposal authority:	s. 30 (1)
Disposal licence:	s. 3 (1)
Holder [of a licence]:	s. 8 (3)
Regulations:	made by the Secretary of State: s. 105 (1)

SUB-S. (1)

A notice should be served under this section in accordance with the provisions of s. 233 of the Local Government Act 1972, which is of general application. An appeal will lie against such a notice: s. 10 (1); and as to cases pending an appeal to the Secretary of State, see s. 10 (2) and (3). A notice of this kind may give rise to a right to compensation on appeal to the Secretary of State: *ibid.*

SUB-S. (4)

"Pollution of water", "danger to public health": see note to s. 5 (3). "Amenities of the locality" is another expression which is incapable of precise definition, but which is in common use. "Amenities" was explained in the old case of *Ellis* v. *Ruislip-Northwood Urban District Council* [1920] 1 K.B. 343, as being "pleasant circumstances or features, advantages".

8. Transfer and relinquishment of licences

(1) The holder of a disposal licence may, after giving notice to the authority which issued the licence that he proposes to transfer it on a day specified in the notice to a person whose name and address are so specified, transfer the licence to that person; but a licence in respect of which such a notice is given shall cease to have effect on the expiration of the period of ten weeks beginning with the date on which the authority receives the notice if during the period of eight weeks beginning with that date the authority gives notice to the transferee that it declines to accept him as the holder of the licence.

(2) If by operation of law the right of the holder of a disposal licence to occupy the relevant land is transferred to some other person, that person shall be deemed to be the holder of the licence during the period of ten weeks beginning with the date of the transfer.

(3) Except as provided by the preceding provisions of this section, references in this Part of this Act to the holder of a disposal licence are references to the person to whom the licence was issued.

(4) The holder of a disposal licence may cancel the licence by delivering it to the authority which issued it and giving notice to the authority that he no longer requires the licence. [29]

DEFINITIONS

Disposal authority:	s. 30 (1)
Disposal licence:	s. 3 (1)
Holder [of a licence]:	sub-s. (3)
Relevant land:	s. 30 (1)

NOTICES

These should be in writing. Whether served by the holder of a licence or by the disposal authority, service should comply with s. 233 of the Local Government Act 1972.

9. Supervision of licensed activities

(1) While a disposal licence is in force it shall be the duty of the authority which issued the licence to take the steps needed—

(*a*) for the purpose of ensuring that the activities to which the licence relates do not cause pollution of water or danger to public health or become seriously detrimental to the amenities of the locality affected by the activities; and

(*b*) for the purpose of ensuring that the conditions specified in the licence are complied with.

(2) For the purpose of performing the duty which is imposed on a disposal authority by the preceding subsection in connection with a licence, any officer of the authority authorised in writing in that behalf by the authority may, if it

appears to him that by reason of an emergency it is necessary to do so, carry out work on the relevant land and on any plant or equipment to which the licence relates.

(3) Where a disposal authority incurs any expenditure by virtue of the preceding subsection, the authority may recover the amount of the expenditure from the holder of the disposal licence in question, or if the licence has been revoked or cancelled from the last holder of it, except where the holder or last holder of the licence shows that there was no emergency requiring any work or except such of the expenditure as he shows was unnecessary.

(4) Where it appears to a disposal authority that a condition specified in a disposal licence issued by the authority is not being complied with, then, without prejudice to any proceedings in pursuance of section 3 or 6 (3) of this Act in consequence of any failure to comply with the condition, the authority may—

- (*a*) serve on the licence holder a notice requiring him to comply with the condition before a time specified in the notice; and
- (*b*) if in the opinion of the authority the licence holder has not complied with the condition by that time, serve on him a further notice revoking the licence at a time specified in the further notice. [**30**]

DEFINITIONS

Disposal authority:	s. 30 (1)
Disposal licence:	s. 3 (1)
Holder [of a licence]:	s. 8 (3)
Relevant land:	s. 30 (1)

SUB-S. (1)

If necessary in order to carry out these duties any person authorised by the authority may enter upon any land or vessel, under s. 91.

SUB-S. (3)

Establishment charges may be added to the expenditure so recoverable under this subsection by virtue of s. 36 of the Local Government Act 1974.

SUB-S. (4)

Service should be effected in accordance with s. 233 of the Local Government Act 1972. As to cases pending an appeal to the Secretary of State, see s. 10 (2) and (3). A notice of this kind may give rise to a right to compensation on an appeal to the Secretary of State: *ibid.*

10. Appeals to Secretary of State from decisions with respect to licences

(1) Where—

- (*a*) an application for a disposal licence or a modification of a disposal licence is rejected; or
- (*b*) a disposal licence which specifies conditions is issued; or
- (*c*) the conditions specified in a disposal licence are modified; or
- (*d*) a disposal licence is revoked,

the applicant for the licence or, as the case may be, the holder or last holder of it may, in accordance with regulations, appeal from the decision in question to the Secretary of State; and where on such an appeal the Secretary of State determines that the decision is to be altered it shall be the duty of the disposal authority concerned to give effect to the determination.

(2) While an appeal in pursuance of the preceding subsection is pending in a case falling within paragraph (*c*) or (*d*) of that subsection, the decision in question shall, subject to the following subsection, be ineffective; and if the appeal is dismissed or withdrawn the decision shall be effective again from the end of the day on which the appeal is dismissed or withdrawn.

(3) The preceding subsection shall not apply to a decision of a disposal authority as respects which the notice relating to the decision which was served on the holder of the relevant licence in pursuance of section 7 or section 9 (4) (*b*) of this Act includes a statement that in the opinion of the authority it is necessary for the purpose of preventing pollution of water or danger to public health that the preceding subsection should not apply to the decision: but if on the application of the holder or former holder of the relevant licence the Secretary of State determines that the authority acted unreasonably in including such a statement in the said notice, then—

(*a*) if the appeal in question is still pending at the end of the day on which the determination is made, the preceding subsection shall apply to the decision from the end of that day; and

(*b*) the holder or former holder of the licence shall be entitled to recover compensation from the authority in respect of any loss suffered by him in consequence of the statement;

and any dispute as to a person's entitlement to compensation in pursuance of paragraph (*b*) of this subsection or as to the amount of the compensation shall be determined by arbitration. [**31**]

DEFINITIONS

Disposal authority:	s. 30 (1)
Disposal licence:	s. 3 (1)
Holder [of a licence]:	s. 8 (3)
Regulations:	made by the Secretary of State: s. 105 (1)

SUB-S. (1)

As to applications for a disposal licence, see s. 5 (1), and as to the revocation of a disposal licence, see s. 7 (1). The power to impose conditions is contained in s. 6, subject to regulations made by the Secretary of State. Those conditions may themselves be modified under s. 7 (1), and in certain circumstances it may be the duty of the disposal authority to modify conditions. There does not seem to be an express power to modify a disposal *licence* (in spite of the terms of sub-s. (1) (*a*) of this section), as distinct from a modification of conditions thereby imposed.

As to transfer of licences, see s. 8.

An appeal under (*c*) or (*d*) has the effect of holding in suspense while the appeal is pending, any modification of conditions or revocation of a licence (sub-s. (2)), except in cases under sub-s. (3).

SUB-S. (2)

This does not apply to cases under sub-s. (3).

SUB-S. (3)

This is the only case where compensation may become payable under this Act, and no special provision has been included elsewhere in the Act for the assessment of the compensation. As no other provision is made, any arbitration will be subject to the provisions of the Arbitration Act 1950; see s. 31 (1) thereof.

11. Special provisions for land occupied by disposal authorities

(1) Nothing in subsection (1) of section 3 of this Act shall apply to—

(*a*) the deposit of controlled waste on land in the area of a disposal authority which is occupied by the authority; or

(*b*) the use on land so occupied of any plant or equipment for the purpose of disposing of controlled waste or of dealing with controlled waste in a manner prescribed in pursuance of paragraph (*b*) of that subsection,

if the deposit is made or the plant or equipment is used by the authority or is made or used with the consent of the authority and in accordance with the conditions, if any, to which the consent is subject (other than a condition as to which it is provided by regulations that the condition shall be disregarded for the purposes of this subsection).

(2) If any land occupied by a disposal authority is used by the authority as a site on which to deposit or permit other persons to deposit controlled waste or on which to use or permit other persons to use any plant or equipment for the purpose aforesaid, it shall be the duty of the authority to ensure that the land is used in accordance with conditions which are—

(*a*) calculated to prevent its use from causing pollution of water, danger to public health and serious detriment to the amenities of the locality in which the land is situated; and

(*b*) specified in a resolution passed by the authority in accordance with the following provisions of this section.

(3) Where a disposal authority proposes that any land which the authority occupies or intends to occupy should be used by the authority as mentioned in the preceding subsection, it shall be the duty of the authority before it gives effect to the proposal—

(*a*) to prepare a statement of the conditions which the authority intends to specify in a resolution to be passed by the authority in pursuance of paragraph (*e*) of this subsection;

(*b*) to include in or, as the case may be, exclude from the statement any condition which by virtue of section 6 (1) of this Act is required to be included in or excluded from a disposal licence;

(*c*) to refer the proposal and the statement to each water authority and collection authority of which the area includes any of the land in question and to any other prescribed person;

(*d*) to consider any representations about the proposal and statement which, during the period of twenty-one days beginning with that on which the proposal and statement are received by a water authority or collection authority or during such longer period as the disposal authority and the other authority agree in writing, the disposal authority receives from the other authority (including in particular any representations about the conditions which the other authority considers should be included in any resolution passed in pursuance of the following paragraph);

(*e*) subject to subsection (5) of this section, to pass a resolution specifying the conditions in accordance with which the land in question is to be used by the disposal authority as mentioned in the preceding subsection.

(4) [*Applies to Scotland only.*]

(5) If a water authority or, in Scotland, a river purification authority to

which a proposal is referred by a disposal authority in pursuance of paragraph (*c*) of subsection (3) of this section requests the disposal authority not to proceed with the proposal or disagrees with the disposal authority as to the conditions to be specified in a resolution in pursuance of paragraph (*e*) of that subsection, either of them may refer the matter to the Secretary of State and it shall be the duty of the disposal authority not to pass a resolution in pursuance of that paragraph except in accordance with his decision.

(6) A disposal authority by which a resolution has been passed in pursuance of paragraph (*e*) of subsection (3) of this section or this subsection—

(*a*) may vary or rescind the resolution by a subsequent resolution of the authority; and

(*b*) shall so vary the resolution when it is necessary to do so in order to secure that the conditions specified in the resolution include or, as the case may be, exclude a condition which by virtue of section 6 (1) of this Act is required to be included in or excluded from a disposal licence.

(7) Paragraphs (*a*) to (*d*) of subsection (3) and subsection (5) of this section shall with the necessary modifications apply to a proposal to pass a resolution in pursuance of paragraph (*a*) of the preceding subsection and to such a resolution as they apply to such a proposal as is mentioned in those provisions and to a resolution in pursuance of the said paragraph (*e*), except that—

(*a*) those provisions shall not apply to or to a proposal to pass a resolution which only rescinds a previous resolution; and

(*b*) the disposal authority may postpone the reference in pursuance of the said subsection (3) so far as the authority considers that by reason of an emergency it is appropriate to do so; and

(*c*) the disposal authority may disregard any other authority for the purposes of the preceding provisions of this subsection in relation to a resolution which, in the opinion of the disposal authority, will not affect the other authority.

(8) If while a resolution is in force in pursuance of the preceding provisions of this section it appears to the authority which passed the resolution—

(*a*) that the continuation of activities to which the resolution relates would cause pollution of water or danger to public health or would be so seriously detrimental to the amenities of the locality affected by the activities that the activities ought not to continue; and

(*b*) that the pollution, danger or detriment cannot be avoided by modifying the conditions relating to the carrying on of the activities,

it shall be the duty of the authority to discontinue the activities and to rescind the resolution.

(9) If it appears to a water authority or, in Scotland, a river purification authority that activities to which a resolution in pursuance of this section relates are causing or likely to cause pollution to relevant waters (within the meaning of Part II of this Act) in the area of the authority the authority may, without prejudice to the provisions of the preceding subsection or the said Part II, request the Secretary of State to direct the disposal authority which passed the resolution to discontinue the activities; and it shall be the duty of a disposal authority to comply with a direction given to it in pursuance of this subsection.

(10) While a resolution passed by a disposal authority in pursuance of sub-

section (3) or (6) of this section is in force it shall be the duty of the authority to secure that particulars of the resolution are included in the register maintained by the authority in pursuance of section 6 (4) (*a*) of this Act.

(11) References to land in this section include such water as is mentioned in section 4 (4) of this Act. [**32**]

DEFINITIONS

Collection authority:	s. 30 (1)
Controlled waste:	s. 30 (1)
Disposal authority:	s. 30 (1)
Disposal licence:	s. 3 (1)
Land:	includes water: see sub-s. (11) and s. 4 (4)
Regulations:	made by the Secretary of State: s. 105 (1)
Relevant waters:	see s. 31 (1) (*a*), applied by sub-s. (9)
Waste:	s. 39 (1) and see s. 30 (3)
Water authority:	Water Act 1973, s. 2

GENERAL NOTE

This section in effect applies the controls of Part I to land occupied by a disposal authority. If they propose to set aside land for the disposal of controlled waste by members of the public they pass a special resolution, having first prepared a statement and carried out constultations in accordance with sub-s. (3).

SUB-S. (1)

This refers to land used for waste disposal by the disposal authority themselves; for this (and for land used under sub-s. (2)) they will not need a disposal licence under s. 3 (1), although they may need planning permission. As to conditions which are to be disregarded under regulations, compare s. 6 (1).

SUB-S. (2)

Before land is so used, there must be consultation (see comment on s. 2) with the water authority and the collection authority (sub-s. (3)), and if there is any disagreement, the matter may be referred to the Secretary of State for his determination: sub-s. (6).

SUB-S. (6)

The disposal authority must also rescind the resolution in circumstances falling within sub-s. (8). The Secretary of State may on a request from the water authority direct the disposal authority to discontinue activities carried on pursuant to a resolution under sub-s. (2): see sub-s. (9).

Collection and disposal of controlled waste

12. Collection of waste

(1) It shall be the duty of each collection authority—

(*a*) subject to subsection (3) of this section, to arrange for the collection of all household waste in its area except waste—

(i) which is situated at a place which in the opinion of the authority is so isolated or inaccessible that the cost of collecting it would be unreasonably high, and

(ii) as to which the authority is satisfied that adequate arrangements for its disposal have been or can reasonably be expected to be made by a person who controls the waste; and

(*b*) if requested by the occupier of premises in its area to collect any commercial waste from the premises, to arrange for the collection of the waste.

(2) Each English disposal authority and each collection authority may, if requested by the occupier of premises in its area to collect any industrial waste from the premises, arrange for the collection of the waste; but an English collection authority shall not be entitled to exercise the powers conferred on it by this subsection except with the consent of the relevant disposal authority.

(3) No charge shall be made for the collection of household waste in pursuance of the preceding provisions of this section except in prescribed cases; and in any of those cases—

(*a*) the duty to arrange for the collection of the waste in question which is imposed on the collection authority by subsection (1) (*a*) of this section shall not arise until a person who controls the waste requests the authority to collect it; and

(*b*) the authority may recover a reasonable charge for the collection of the waste from the person who made the request in respect of it in pursuance of the preceding paragraph.

(4) A person at whose request waste other than household waste is collected in pursuance of the preceding provisions of this section shall be liable to pay a reasonable charge for the collection and disposal of the waste to the authority which arranged for its collection; and it shall be the duty of that authority to recover the charge unless in the case of a charge in respect of commercial waste the authority considers it inappropriate to do so.

(5) It shall be the duty of each collection authority—

(*a*) to make such arrangements for the emptying of privies serving one or more private dwellings in its area as the authority considers appropriate and to make no charge for emptying done in pursuance of the arrangements;

(*b*) if requested by the person who controls a cesspool serving only one or more private dwellings in its area to empty the cesspool, to remove such of the contents of the cesspool as the authority considers appropriate on payment if the authority so requires of a reasonable charge;

and a collection authority may, if requested by the person who controls any other privy or cesspool in its area to empty the privy or cesspool, remove matter from it on payment as aforesaid.

In this subsection "privy" means a latrine which has a moveable receptacle for faecal matter and "cesspool" includes a settlement tank or other tank for the reception or disposal of foul matter from buildings.

(6) An English disposal authority and any collection authority may—

(*a*) construct, lay and maintain, within or outside its area, pipes and associated works for the purpose of collecting waste in pursuance of this section;

(*b*) contribute towards the cost incurred by another person in providing or maintaining pipes or associated works connecting with pipes provided by the authority in pursuance of the preceding paragraph.

(7) Parts V and VI of Schedule 3 to the Water Act 1945 (which relate to the laying of mains and the breaking up of streets) shall apply in relation to pipes and associated works provided or to be provided in pursuance of paragraph (*a*) of the preceding subsection as those Parts apply in relation to water mains and pipes but as if—

(*a*) sections 19 (4) and 21 of that Schedule (which relate to the erection of street notices and the laying of service pipes) were omitted, and in section 22 of that Schedule the words "which they are authorised to lay" were omitted; and

(*b*) for any reference to undertakers or limits of supply there were substituted respectively a reference to the authority in question and the area of the authority; and

(*c*) for the reference to the special Act in section 25 (4) of that Schedule there were substituted a reference to this subsection;

and the Pipe-lines Act 1962 shall not apply to pipes or associated works provided or to be provided in pursuance of paragraph (*a*) of the preceding subsection.

(8) A collection authority may contribute towards the cost incurred by another person in providing or maintaining plant or equipment intended to deal with household waste before it is collected under arrangements made by the authority in pursuance of subsection (1) (*a*) of this section; and an English disposal authority and any collection authority may contribute towards the cost incurred by another person in providing or maintaining plant or equipment intended to deal with commercial or industrial waste before it is collected under arrangements made by the authority in pursuance of subsection (1) (*b*) or subsection (2) of this section.

(9) Subject to section 14 (1) and (9) of this Act, anything collected under arrangements made by an authority in pursuance of this section shall belong to the authority and may be dealt with accordingly.

(10) [*Applies to Scotland only.*]

(11) References to waste in the preceding provisions of this section include waste on premises occupied by the Crown but exclude waste as to which the Commissioners executing the Crown Estate Paving Act 1851 (which among other things relates to premises in the Regent's Park) make arrangements for its collection; but a disposal or collection authority shall not be entitled by virtue of this subsection to exercise, in relation to such premises or waste on such premises, any power conferred on the authority by virtue of sections 91 to 93 of this Act. [**33**]

DEFINITIONS

Cesspool:	in sub-s. (5); see that subsection
Collection authority:	s. 30 (1)
Commercial waste:	s. 30 (3)
English disposal authority:	s. 30 (1)
Household waste:	s. 30 (3)
Industrial waste:	s. 30 (3)
Premises:	see s. 105 (1)
Prescribed:	by regulations made by the Secretary of State: s. 105 (1)
Private dwelling:	s. 30 (1)
Privy:	in sub-s. (4): see that subsection
Waste:	s. 30 (1) and see s. 30 (3)

GENERAL NOTE

This is the substantive section that replaces ss. 72–74 of the Public Health Act 1936; it will be noted that local authorities no longer have powers to make byelaws relating to the collection of waste but provisions much to the same effect may be included in regulations made under s. 13 (7). Household waste must be collected free of charge from all premises in the area of a collection authority, and "premises" is so defined (in s. 105 (1)) as to include caravan sites and houseboats permanently moored to land (see *West Mersea Urban District Council* v. *Fraser*, [1950] 1 All E.R. 990). Commercial waste must be collected on request, and industrial waste *may* be so collected, but in the latter case in England the collection authority must obtain the consent of the disposal authority (sub-s. (2)). No charge may be made for the collection of household waste, except as may be prescribed in regulations (and then only on request from the person controlling the waste), but in other cases the authority are under a duty to collect a "reasonable" charge, unless in the case of commercial waste they consider a charge would be inappropriate (sub-s. (3)).

It will be noted that the expressions "house refuse", "trade refuse" and "other refuse" used in the Public Health Act 1936 have been abandoned in favour of "household, commercial and industrial waste", each defined in s. 30 (3). For a recent explanation of "house refuse", see *Iron Trades Mutual Employers Insurance Association, Ltd.* v. *Sheffield Corporation*, [1974] 1 All E.R. 182. Collection authorities are also under a duty to arrange for privy emptying from private dwellings without charge, and to remove the contents of cesspools serving private dwellings on request at a reasonable charge (sub-s. (4)). They also have a *power* to empty other privies and cesspools (*ibid.*). Subsection (6) introduces a new civil engineering concept, in that it enables waste to be collected in pipes (and see p. 28). As to the sorting over, etc., of dustbins, this is made an offence by s. 27. As to financial arrangements between collection and disposal authorities, see s. 14 (7) and (8).

SUB-S. (1)

The collection authority are no longer liable to a "common informer" penalty if they fail to collect household waste weekly (see Public Health Act 1936, s. 72 (2)), but the Secretary of State could be asked to use his default powers in an appropriate case (see s. 97 of this Act).

SUB-S. (2)

In Wales the collection authority is also the disposal authority. The subsection also applies to waste other than controlled waste: s. 18 (3).

SUB-S. (3)

"Reasonable charge": this may include establishment expenses of the local authority: Local Government Act 1974, s. 36.

SUB-S. (5)

"Reasonable charge": see sub-s. (3), *supra*. "Latrine" is not defined.

SUB-S. (6)

This subsection may also be used in connection with the conveyance of heat, etc.: see s. 21 (4). A map of the pipes must be prepared: s. 28, and see also s. 14 (5) and sub-s. (7) of this section.

SUB-S. (7)

See s. 14 (5).

SUB-S. (9)

"Waste" is defined non-exclusively in s. 30 (1), but it is reasonably clear that only those items left by the former owner for the purpose of collection by the collection authority, or clearly abandoned by him, are properly "waste". Therefore it would seem that an article of value (e.g. jewellery) inadvertently placed in a dustbin for collection still belongs to the original owner of such an article, in spite of the present subsection. On the other hand, ownership would probably pass if all reasonable efforts to trace the original owner have been carried out without success. The subsection does, however, make it clear that the servants of the collection authority cannot acquire ownership by taking possession of any waste: any such action would seem to amount to theft: see *Williams* v. *Phillips* (1957), 41 Cr. App. Rep. 5. When waste collected by the collection authority has been delivered to the disposal authority, it will belong to the latter authority (s. 14 (1)), but until such delivery (or other disposal, such as the sale of waste paper) the waste will remain the property of the collection authority. It is made clear by s. 20 (*c*) that waste acquired by a disposal authority may be sold for re-cycling.

SUB-S. (11)

As there is no specific provision to that effect, the Act does not in general apply to premises occupied by the Crown: but the Act does apply to certain interests in Crown land: see s. 105 (3).

13. Dustbins, etc.

(1) Where a collection authority has a duty by virtue of subsection (1) (*a*) of the preceding section to arrange for the collection of household waste from any premises, then, subject to any regulations made by virtue of subsection (7) of this section, the authority may, by a notice served on the occupier of the premises, require him to place the waste for collection in receptacles which are of a kind and number reasonably specified in the notice; and a person who fails to comply with such a requirement shall be guilty of an offence and liable on summary conviction to a fine of an amount not exceeding £100.

(2) A notice served by an authority in pursuance of the preceding subsection may provide for the receptacles in question to be provided by the authority free of charge or—

(*a*) if the recipient of the notice agrees, by the authority on payment by the recipient of the notice of such a single payment or such periodical payments as he agrees with the authority; or

(*b*) by the recipient of the notice if he does not enter into an agreement in pursuance of the preceding paragraph within a period specified in the notice or the notice does not propose such an agreement.

(3) Where by virtue of such a notice the recipient of it is required to provide any receptacles he may within the period of twenty-one days beginning with the last day of the period specified in the notice in pursuance of paragraph (*b*) of the preceding subsection or, where no period is so specified, beginning with the day on which the notice is served on him, appeal to a magistrates' court against the notice on the ground that the kind or number of the receptacles required by the notice is unreasonable or on the ground that the receptacles in which household waste in the premises in question is placed for collection are adequate; and where an appeal against a notice is brought in pursuance of this subsection—

(*a*) the notice shall be of no effect pending the determination of the appeal; and

(*b*) the court shall either quash or modify the notice or dismiss the appeal; and

(*c*) no question as to whether the kind or number of receptacles specified in the notice is unreasonable shall be entertained in any proceedings for an offence under this section in respect of the notice.

(4) An English disposal authority and any collection authority may at the request of any person supply him with receptacles for commercial waste or industrial waste which he has requested the authority to arrange to collect and shall make a reasonable charge for any receptacle supplied in pursuance of this subsection unless in the case of a receptacle for commercial waste the authority considers it appropriate not to make a charge.

(5) If it appears to a collection authority that there is likely to be situated, on any premises in its area, commercial waste or industrial waste of a kind which, if the waste is not stored in receptacles of a particular kind, is likely to cause a nusiance or to be detrimental to the amenities of the locality in which the premises are situated, the authority may, by a notice served on the occupier of the premises, require him to provide at the premises receptacles for the storage of such waste which, subject to subsection (7) of this section, are of a kind and number reasonably specified in the notice; and a person who fails to comply with such a requirement shall be guilty of an offence and liable on summary conviction to a fine of an amount not exceeding £100.

(6) A person on whom a notice is served in pursuance of the preceding subsection may, within the period of twenty-one days beginning with the day on which the notice is served on him, appeal to a magistrates' court against the notice on the grounds that the kind or number of receptacles specified in the notice is unreasonable or that the waste is not likely to cause a nuisance or be detrimental to the amenities of the locality in which the premises are situated; and where an appeal against a notice is brought in pursuance of this subsection, paragraphs (*a*) to (*c*) of subsection (3) of this section shall apply in relation to the notice as they apply in relation to such a notice as is mentioned in that subsection.

(7) Provision may be made by regulations with respect to—

(*a*) the size, construction and maintenance of receptacles for controlled waste;

(*b*) the placing of the receptacles on premises for the purpose of facilitating the emptying of them, and access to the receptacles for that purpose;

(*c*) the placing of the receptacles for that purpose on highways with the consent of the relevant highway authorities and the liability for any damage arising out of the placing of the receptacles on highways in pursuance of regulations made by virtue of this subsection;

(*d*) the substances which may and may not be put into the receptacles and the precautions to be taken where particular substances are put into them;

(*e*) the steps to be taken by occupiers of premises for the purpose of facilitating the collection of waste from receptacles for controlled waste which are provided in connection with the premises;

(*f*) the giving of directions by collection authorities with respect to matters mentioned in any of the preceding paragraphs and compliance with the directions by occupiers of premises and other persons; and (*g*) the imposition of a fine of an amount not exceeding £100 on summary conviction of a contravention of the regulations or directions given in pursuance of the regulations.

(8) References to receptacles in the preceding provisions of this section include references to holders for receptacles. [**34**]

DEFINITIONS

Collection authority:	s. 30 (1)
Commercial waste:	s. 30 (3)
Controlled waste:	s. 30 (1)
English disposal authority:	s. 30 (1)
Household waste:	s. 30 (3)
Industrial waste:	s. 30 (3)
Premises:	s. 105 (1)
Receptacles:	sub-s. (8)
Regulations:	made by the Secretary of State: s. 105 (1)

GENERAL NOTE

This section replaces and very considerably clarifies the law formerly contained in s. 75 of the Public Health Act 1936 (repealed: see Sch. 4). Householders can be required to place household waste in specified receptacles (an expression which, it is made clear in sub-s. (8), includes a holder to take a sack or other receptacle) in accordance with sub-s. (1) and regulations made under sub-s. (7); sub-s. (2) empowers the authority to provide the receptacle(s) either free, or on payment of an agreed charge. The former clumsy system of collecting an extra 37½p on the annual rate demand has been abolished. The recipient of such a notice may appeal to the magistrates under sub-s. (3); provided the notice has been served on the occupier there can be no dispute under this section as to whether the correct person has been served with the notice, as arose in such cases as *Croydon Corporation* v. *Thomas*, [1947] K.B. 386; [1947] 1 All E.R. 239, and *First National Housing Trust, Ltd.* v. *Chesterfield Rural District Council* [1948] 2 K.B. 351; [1948] 2 All E.R. 658. Subsections (4), (5) and (6) are concerned with receptacles for commercial or industrial waste.

SUB-S. (1)

Note that the subsection applies only in cases where s. 12 (1) (*a*) imposes a duty. Because of the definition of household waste in s. 30 (3), "premises" should not be read as meaning only private dwellings. The notice should be served in accordance with s. 233 of the Local Government Act 1972. "Occupier" is not defined in the Act, and is not necessarily confined to the "rateable occupier", but seems to mean the responsible person in *de facto* occupation of the premises. There is a right of appeal against the notice under sub-s. (3), within 21 days of the end of any compliance period specified in the notice, or the date of service.

SUB-S. (2)

The authority cannot insist on the payment of a charge, but they can require the occupier to provide a receptacle of a kind reasonably specified in the notice. An appeal will lie under sub-s. (3) on a question as to the reasonableness of the kind of bin specified, but this point could not be raised by way of a defence on a prosecution brought under sub-s. (1).

SUB-S. (3)

Paragraphs (*a*) to (*c*) will apply also to an appeal under sub-s. (6).

SUB-S. (4)

The "reasonable" charge may include an element for establishment expenses: Local Government Act 1974, s. 36. The subsection also applies to waste other than controlled waste: s. 18 (3).

SUB-S. (5)

As to "amenities", see note to s. 7 (4). As to service of the notice, see note to sub-s. (1) above.

SUB-S. (7)

These regulations will replace byelaws made under s. 72 (3) and (4) of the Public Health Act 1936. Any such byelaws ceased to have effect on the repeal by Sch. 4 of those subsections.

Hitherto the placing of a dustbin on a highway for any considerable time has probably amounted to an obstruction (see *Wandsworth Corporation* v. *Baines*, [1906] 1 K.B. 470), and this still seems to be the case if a bin is deposited on a highway otherwise than in accordance with the regulations under this subsection.

14. Disposal of waste in England and Wales

(1) Subject to the following subsection, it shall be the duty of each English collection authority to deliver to the relevant disposal authority, at such places as the disposal authority directs, all waste which is collected by the collection authority in pursuance of section 12 of this Act except waste paper which the collection authority decides is not to be delivered to the disposal authority; and anything delivered to a disposal authority in pursuance of this subsection shall belong to that authority and may be dealt with accordingly.

(2) An English collection authority and the relevant disposal authority may agree that, subject to such conditions as to payment or otherwise as may be specified in the agreement, waste to which the agreement relates shall not be delivered to the disposal authority in pursuance of the preceding subsection but shall be dealt with under arrangements made by the collection authority for the purpose of enabling the waste to be used again or substances to be reclaimed from it.

(3) Without prejudice to the powers of collection authorities apart from this subsection, a collection authority shall have power to provide plant and equipment for the sorting and baling of waste paper retained by the authority in pursuance of subsection (1) of this section or for sorting or processing waste retained by the authority in pursuance of the preceding subsection.

(4) It shall be the duty of each disposal authority to arrange for the disposal of the waste collected by it in pursuance of section 12 of this Act or delivered to it in pursuance of subsection (1) of this section; and, without prejudice to the authority's powers apart from the following provisions of this subsection, the powers exercisable by the authority for the purpose of performing that duty shall include power—

(*a*) to provide, within or outside its area, places at which to deposit waste before the authority transfers it to a place or plant or equipment provided in pursuance of the following paragraph; and

(*b*) to provide, within or outside its area, places at which to dispose of the waste and plant or equipment for processing it or otherwise disposing of it.

(5) Subsections (6) and (7) of section 12 of this Act shall have effect in relation to a disposal authority as if the reference in paragraph (*a*) of the said subsection (6) to the collection of waste in pursuance of that section included the disposal of waste in pursuance of this section and the disposal of anything produced from waste belonging to the authority.

(6) A disposal authority or a collection authority may permit another person to use facilities provided by the authority in pursuance of the preceding provisions of this section and may provide for the use of another person any such facilities as the authority has power to provide in pursuance of those provisions; and—

(*a*) subject to the following paragraph, it shall be the duty of the authority to make a reasonable charge in respect of the use by another person of the facilities unless the authority considers it appropriate not to make a charge;

(*b*) no charge shall be made in pursuance of this subsection in respect of household waste; and

(*c*) anything delivered to the authority by another person in the course of using the facilities shall belong to the authority and may be dealt with accordingly.

(7) A collection authority and the relevant disposal authority may enter into an agreement for the making by either authority to the other of such payments as may be determined by or under the agreement in respect of waste collected by the collection authority in pursuance of section 12 of this Act including, without prejudice to the generality of the preceding provisions of this subsection, an agreement for the making of payments to the collection authority in respect of such arrangements as are mentioned in subsection (2) of this section.

(8) Except as otherwise agreed in pursuance of the preceding subsection, the relevant disposal authority shall—

(*a*) be entitled to receive from an English collection authority such sums as are needed to defray the reasonable cost to the disposal authority of disposing of commercial and industrial waste delivered to the disposal authority by the collection authority in pursuance of this section; and

(*b*) pay to an English collection authority a reasonable contribution towards expenditure reasonably incurred by the collection authority in delivering waste to the disposal authority in pursuance of subsection (1) of this section where the place of delivery is unreasonably far from the collection authority's area;

and any question arising in pursuance of paragraph (*a*) of this subsection as to what cost is reasonable or in pursuance of paragraph (*b*) of this subsection as to whether a contribution is reasonable or expenditure was reasonably incurred or as to whether a place is unreasonably far from a collection authority's area shall, in default of agreement between the two authorities in question, be determined by arbitration.

(9) References to waste in subsections (1), (2), (4), (7) and (8) of this section do not include matter removed from privies or cesspools in pursuance of section 12 (5) of this Act, and it shall be the duty of a collection authority by which matter is so removed—

(*a*) to deliver the matter, in accordance with any directions of the water authority of which the area includes that of the collection authority, at a place specified in the directions (which must be in or within a reasonable distance from the collection authority's area) to the water authority or to another person so specified;

(*b*) to give to the water authority from time to time a notice stating the quantity of the matter which the collection authority expects to deliver to or as directed by the water authority in pursuance of the preceding paragraph during a period specified in the notice.

(10) Any question arising in pursuance of paragraph (*a*) of the preceding subsection as to whether a place is within a reasonable distance from a collection authority's area shall, in default of agreement between the collection authority and the water authority in question, be determined by arbitration; and anything delivered to a water authority in pursuance of that subsection shall belong to the authority and may be dealt with accordingly.

(11) For the purposes of sections 30 and 31 of the Water Act 1973 (which among other things relate to charges for services performed by water authorities) the reception and disposal by a water authority or other person of matter delivered to it or him by another authority in pursuance of subsection (9) of this section shall be treated as a service performed by the water authority for the other authority.

(12) This section does not apply to Scotland. [**35**]

DEFINITIONS

Cesspool:	s. 12 (5)
Collection authority:	s. 30 (1)
Disposal authority:	s. 30 (1)
English collection authority:	s. 30 (1)
Privy:	s. 12 (5)
Water authority:	Water Act 1973, s. 2

GENERAL NOTE

This section, following the split in the functions of collection and disposal respectively as between districts and counties in England (in Wales the districts perform both functions), introduced by the Local Government Act 1972, provides for collection authorities in England to deliver to disposal authorities, at such places as the latter authority may direct, all waste (of all kinds) except matter removed from privies or cesspools (see sub-s. (9)), collected by them under s. 12 of the Act. The collection authority may decide to keep waste paper for sorting, bailing under sub-s. (3), and then (as the waste is their property (s. 12 (9)) they may sell the paper (s. 20). Other waste can similarly be retained by the collection authority if the disposal authority agrees under sub-s. (2). Financial adjustments between the two authorities fall to be made under sub-ss. (7) and (8).

It is the duty of the disposal authority to arrange for the disposal of waste (sub-s. (4)), and they may arrange for reclamation or re-cycling, but there is no duty on them to do this, nor is there any express duty on them to implement the provisions of their own disposal plan prepared under s. 2.

SUB-S. (1)

As to ownership of waste, see note to s. 12 (9).

SUB-S. (2)

There is no procedure for reference to arbitration or otherwise in the event of one authority failing to agree.

SUB-S. (4)

This power to provide a place for the deposit of waste includes a power to acquire the land compulsorily in accordance with the normal procedure: Local Government Act 1972, ss. 120 and 121. Planning permission will normally be necessary for the opening of a new tip. The tip may be made available for deposit of waste by members of the public subject to payment for other than household waste: sub-s. (6). The duty of a disposal authority to provide a refuse dump for residents and others imposed by s. 18 of the Civic Amenities Act 1967 (as amended by Sch. 14 of the Local Government Act 1972 and Sch. 3 to this Act) is not affected by the present Act.

SUB-S. (6)

See comment on sub-s. (4).

SUB-S. (8)

Any arbitration under this subsection should be conducted in accordance with the provisions of the Arbitration Act 1950 (see s. 31 (1) thereof).

SUB-S. (9)

Service of a notice under this subsection should be effected in accordance with s. 233 of the Local Government Act 1972.

15. [*Applies to Scotland only.*]

16. Removal of waste deposited in breach of licensing provisions

(1) If any controlled waste is deposited on any land in the area of a disposal authority or a collection authority in contravention of section 3 (1) of this Act, the authority may serve a notice on the occupier of the land requiring him—

(*a*) to remove the waste from the land within a period specified in the notice, which shall not be less than twenty-one days beginning with the date of service of the notice; or

(*b*) to take within such a period such steps as are so specified with a view to eliminating or reducing the consequences of the deposit of the waste,

or requiring him both to remove the waste as mentioned in paragraph (*a*) of this subsection and to take such steps as are mentioned in paragraph (*b*) of this subsection within such a period as aforesaid.

(2) A person served with a notice in pursuance of the preceding subsection may within the twenty-one days aforesaid appeal to a magistrates' court against the notice; and on any such appeal the court shall quash the notice if it is satisfied that—

(*a*) the appellant neither deposited nor caused nor knowingly permitted the deposit of the waste on the land; or

(*b*) service of the notice on the appellant was not authorised by the preceding subsection; or

(*c*) there is a material defect in the notice;

and in any other case shall either modify the notice or dismiss the appeal.

(3) Where a person appeals against a notice in pursuance of this section, the notice shall be of no effect pending the determination of the appeal; and where the court modifies the notice or dismisses the appeal it may extend the period specified in the notice.

(4) If a person on whom a notice is served in pursuance of subsection (1) of this section fails to comply with the notice, then—

(*a*) he shall be guilty of an offence and liable on summary conviction to a fine not exceeding £400 and a further fine not exceeding £50 for each day on which the failure continues after conviction for the offence and before the authority which served the notice has begun to exercise its powers in pursuance of the following paragraph; and

(*b*) the said authority may do what that person was required by the notice to do and may recover from him any expenses reasonably incurred by the authority in doing it.

(5) If it appears to such an authority as is mentioned in subsection (1) of this section that waste has been deposited as there mentioned and that—

(*a*) in order to remove or prevent pollution of water or danger to public health it is necessary forthwith to remove the waste or to take other steps with a view to eliminating or reducing the consequences of the deposit of it or necessary forthwith to remove the waste and to take such other steps; or

(*b*) there is no occupier of the land in question; or

(*c*) the occupier of the land neither made nor knowingly permitted the deposit of the waste,

the authority may remove the waste from the land or take such other steps as aforesaid or, as the case may require, may remove it and take such other steps.

(6) Where an authority exercises in respect of any land a power conferred on it by the preceding subsection it shall be entitled to recover the cost of doing so and of disposing of any waste removed in the exercise of the power—

(*a*) in a case falling within paragraph (*a*) of that subsection, from the occupier of the land unless he proves that he neither made nor caused nor knowingly permitted the deposit in question;

(*b*) in any case, from any person who deposited or caused or knowingly permitted the deposit of any of the waste in question on the land,

except such of the cost as the occupier or other person shows was incurred unnecessarily.

(7) Any waste removed by an authority in pursuance of this section shall belong to the authority and may be dealt with accordingly. [**36**]

DEFINITIONS

Collection authority:	s. 30 (1)
Controlled waste:	s. 30 (1)
Disposal authority:	s. 30 (1)
Waste:	s. 30 (1) and see s. 30 (3)

GENERAL NOTE

This section deals with the removal of waste deposited on land otherwise than in accordance with the terms of a disposal licence or as may be otherwise authorised. The substantive offence is created by ss. 3 (3) and 3 (4), but this section enables the authority to take remedial action.

SUB-S. (1)

A notice should be served in accordance with s. 233 of the Local Government Act 1972.

SUB-S. (2)

"Caused or knowingly permitted": see note to s. 31 (1).

SUB-S. (6)

Establishment expenses of the local authority may be recovered as part of the actual cost: Local Government Act 1974, s. 36.

SUB-S. (7)

As to ownership of waste, see note to s. 12 (9).

17. Special provisions with respect to certain dangerous or intractable waste

(1) If the Secretary of State considers that controlled waste of any kind is or may be so dangerous or difficult to dispose of that special provision in pursuance of this subsection is required for the disposal of waste of that kind by disposal authorities or other persons, it shall be his duty to make provision by regulations for the disposal of waste of that kind (hereafter in this section referred to as "special waste"); and, without prejudice to the generality of the Secretary of State's power to make regulations in pursuance of the preceding provisions of this subsection, any such regulations may include provision—

(*a*) for the giving of directions by disposal authorities with respect to matters connected with the disposal of special waste;

(*b*) for securing that special waste is not, while awaiting disposal in pursuance of the regulations, kept at any one place in quantities greater than those which are prescribed and in circumstances which differ from those which are prescribed;

(*c*) for requiring the occupier of premises on which special waste is situated to give notice of that fact and other prescribed information to a prescribed authority;

(*d*) for the keeping of records by persons who produce or dispose of special waste or transfer it to another person for disposal, for the inspection of the records and for the furnishing by such persons to prescribed authorities of copies of or information derived from the records;

(*e*) providing that a contravention of the regulations shall be an offence and prescribing the maximum penalty for the offence (which shall not exceed, on summary conviction, a fine of £400 and, on conviction on indictment, imprisonment for a term of two years and a fine).

(2) Without prejudice to the generality of the power to make regulations conferred by the preceding subsection, regulations made in pursuance of that subsection may include provision—

(*a*) requiring special waste of particular kinds to be disposed of only by disposal authorities or, in the case of special waste of a kind which the Secretary of State considers involves or may involve such a risk of damage to persons or animals or vegetation that it should be disposed of only by him, to be disposed of only by the Secretary of State;

(*b*) for the supervision by disposal authorities (whether by the application with modifications of provisions of section 9 of this Act or otherwise) of activities authorised by virtue of the regulations;

(*c*) as to the recovery of expenses or other charges for disposals by disposal authorities or the Secretary of State in pursuance of the regulations;

(*d*) as to appeals to the Secretary of State from decisions of disposal authorities in pursuance of the regulations.

(3) Provision may also be made by regulations—

(*a*) for the giving of a direction, in respect of any place in respect of which a disposal licence or a resolution in pursuance of section 11 of this Act is in force, requiring the holder of the licence or the authority which passed the resolution to accept and dispose of at the place, on such terms as are specified in the direction (including terms as to the making of payments to the recipient of the direction), such special waste as is so specified;

(*b*) as to the consents to be obtained and the other steps to be taken before a direction may be given in pursuance of the regulations and as to appeals to the Secretary of State against a direction so given;

(*c*) providing that a failure to comply with such a direction shall be an offence punishable on summary conviction by a fine not exceeding £400 or such less amount as is prescribed and that a person shall not be guilty of an offence under any prescribed enactment by reason only of anything necessarily done or omitted in order to comply with such a direction. **[37]**

DEFINITIONS

Controlled waste:	s. 30 (1)
Disposal authority:	s. 30 (1)
Disposal licence:	s. 3 (1)
Premises:	s. 105 (1)
Regulations:	made by the Secretary of State under s. 104 and see s. 105 (1)
"Special" waste:	sub-s. (1)
Waste:	s. 30 (1) and see s. 30 (3)

GENERAL NOTE

This section empowers the Secretary of State to make very wide ranging regulations in respect of the disposal, etc., of waste which he considers to be of a kind that is or may be so dangerous or difficult to dispose of that special provision is required. It is to be hoped that these powers, together with the other powers of the Act, will be used so as to require the provision of places where special waste (as it is called in this section) *may* be deposited, and that the powers are not only used to prevent the deposit of "special waste" in unsuitable places.

Waste other than controlled waste

18. Application of preceding provisions to other waste

(1) The Secretary of State may, after consultation with such bodies as he considers appropriate, make regulations providing that prescribed provisions of sections 1 to 11 and 14 to 17 of this Act shall have effect in a prescribed area—

(*a*) as if references in those provisions to controlled waste or controlled waste of a kind specified in the regulations included references to such waste as is mentioned in section 30 (3) (*c*) (ii) of this Act which is of a kind so specified; and

(*b*) with such other modifications as are prescribed;

and regulations made in pursuance of this subsection may make such modifications of any enactment other than the sections aforesaid as the Secretary of State considers appropriate in connection with the regulations.

(2) A person who—

(*a*) deposits on any land any waste other than controlled waste; or

(*b*) causes or knowingly permits the deposit on any land of any waste other than controlled waste,

in a case where, if the waste were controlled waste and any disposal licence relating to the land were not in force, he would be guilty of an offence under section 3 (3) of this Act shall be guilty of such an offence and punishable accordingly unless the act charged was done in pursuance of and in accordance with the terms of any consent, licence, approval or authority granted under any enactment (excluding any planning permission under the enactments relating to town and country planning); and in this subsection "land" includes such water as is mentioned in section 4 (4) of this Act.

(3) Subsection (2) of section 12 and subsection (4) of section 13 of this Act shall apply to waste other than controlled waste as the subsections apply to controlled waste. [**38**]

DEFINITIONS

Controlled waste:	s. 30 (1)
Disposal licence:	s. 3 (1)
Mine:	s. 105 (1)
Prescribed:	by regulations made by the Secretary of State: s. 105 (1)
Quarry:	s. 105 (1)
Waste:	s. 30 (1) and see s. 30 (3)

GENERAL NOTE

This section enables the Secretary of State to make regulations extending the substantive provisions of Part I (other than those concerned with the collection of waste) to specified waste from a mine or quarry. The deposit of waste other than controlled waste on land is dealt with in sub-s. (2).

SUB-S. (1)

Regulations made under this subsection are (exceptionally) not subject to the affirmative resolution procedure in each House of Parliament: s. 104 (2).

SUB-S. (2)

"Causes or knowingly permits": see note to s. 31 (1). As to civil liability in respect of damage sustained in circumstances referred to in this subsection, see s. 88 (1). The time limit within which proceedings for a summary offence may be taken by virtue of this subsection is one year: s. 87 (3).

19. Powers of disposal authorities as respects other waste

Each disposal authority shall have power to collect information about, and to make arrangements for the disposal of, waste which is situated or likely to be situated in its area and is not controlled waste; but nothing in sections 91 to 94 of this Act shall apply to functions conferred on an authority or information collected by an authority in pursuance of this section. [**39**]

DEFINITIONS

Controlled waste:	s. 30 (1)
Disposal authority:	s. 25 (1), s. 30 (1)
Waste:	s. 30 (1), and see s. 30 (3)

GENERAL NOTE

The authority does not have a power of entry on land for this purpose: s. 91. Section 94 refers to the disclosure of trade secrets.

Reclamation, etc., of waste

20. Reclamation of waste

Without prejudice to the powers of disposal authorities apart from this section, any disposal authority may—

(*a*) do such things as the authority considers appropriate for the purpose of—

(i) enabling waste belonging to the authority, or belonging to another person who requests the authority to deal with it in pursuance of this section, to be used again, or

(ii) enabling substances to be reclaimed from such waste;

(*b*) buy or otherwise acquire waste with a view to its being used again or to the reclamation of substances from it; and

(*c*) use, sell or otherwise dispose of waste belonging to the authority or anything produced from such waste. [**40**]

DEFINITIONS

Disposal authority:	s. 30 (1)
Waste:	s. 30 (1) and see s. 30 (3)

GENERAL NOTE

As to the ownership of waste, see note to s. 12 (9). Waste "belongs" to a disposal authority when it has been delivered to them by the collection authority: s. 14 (1).

21. Production of heat and electricity from waste, etc.

(1) A disposal authority may, subject to subsections (2) and (3) of this section,—

(*a*) use waste belonging to the authority for the purpose of producing from it heat or electricity or both;

(*b*) establish and operate, within or outside its area, such generating stations and other installations as the authority thinks fit for the purpose aforesaid; and

(*c*) where the authority operates an installation in which waste is usually used as the main fuel for the purpose of producing heat or electricity, then—

(i) in the case of an installation for producing heat, use other fuel in addition to waste to produce the heat, and

(ii) in the case of an installation for producing electricity, use other fuel to assist in burning the waste to produce the electricity,

and, in an emergency, use other fuel instead of waste to produce the heat or electricity;

and a disposal authority may use, sell or otherwise dispose of any heat produced by the authority by virtue of this section.

(2) A disposal authority shall not be entitled to make any arrangements with a view to the production from waste of electricity for use otherwise than by the authority unless—

(*a*) the authority has had consultations about the arrangements with the Central Electricity Generating Board and with any Electricity Board proposed to be specified in the arrangements in pursuance of paragraph (*b*) of the following subsection; and (*b*) the arrangements are approved by the Secretary of State and are in accordance with any conditions which he attaches to his approval.

. . . . .

(3) Where a disposal authority produces electricity by virtue of this section the authority—

(*a*) may use any of the electricity at the installation at which it was produced and on any premises occupied by the authority in connection with the installation, but shall not use any of it elsewhere;

(*b*) may sell any of the electricity, on such terms as are specified in the relevant arrangements made in pursuance of the preceding subsection, to any Electricity Board (within the meaning of the Electricity Act 1947) which is so specified, but shall not sell or otherwise dispose of any of it to any other person;

and it shall be the duty of any Electricity Board so specified to buy electricity from the authority in accordance with the said arrangements.

(4) Subsection (6) of section 12 of this Act (except paragraph (*b*) of that subsection) and subsection (7) of that section (except so much of it as relates to the Pipe-lines Act 1962) shall have effect in relation to a dispoal authority as if the reference in the said subsection (6) to the collection of waste in pursuance of that section included the conveying of heat produced by the authority by virtue of this section and of air, steam and water heated by such heat.

(5) It shall be the duty of a disposal authority by which an installation for producing heat is operated in pursuance of this section in any year to furnish to the Secretary of State, as soon as practicable after the end of that year, such particulars relating to the installation and heat produced at it as are prescribed.

(6) Nothing in this section (except the restrictions imposed by subsections (2) and (3)) shall be construed as prejudicing any power exercisable by a disposal authority apart from this section. [**41**]

DEFINITIONS

Disposal authority:	s. 30 (1)
Waste:	s. 30 (1), and see s. 30 (3)

GENERAL NOTE

This section empowers a disposal authority to use waste to produce heat and to use the heat so produced for their own premises, or they may sell or otherwise dispose of the heat subject only to making an annual report to the Secretary of State: sub-s. (5). They may also use waste to produce electricity and may use the electricity at the installation where it was produced or on other premises occupied by them in connection with the installation. If, however, they propose to use the electricity in some other manner, they must have consultations with the Central Electricity Generating Board and the Area Electricity Board, and they must make arrangements approved by the Secretary of State. Electricity may be sold pursuant to these arrangements only to an Electricity Board, and it will be the Board's duty to buy the electricity.

SUB-S. (1)

As to ownership of waste, see s. 12 (9) and s. 14 (1).

SUB-S. (4)

Section 12 (6) empowers the disposal authority to lay cables, mains, etc., and they may break open streets for the purpose under s. 12 (7). They will be obliged to prepare maps of such cables, etc., under s. 28 (1).

Street cleaning and litter

22. Street cleaning, etc.

(1) It shall be the duty of each highway authority to undertake the cleaning of the highways for which it is the highway authority so far as the cleaning of the highways is necessary for the maintenance of the highways or the safety of traffic on them.

(2) It shall be the duty of each local authority to undertake the cleaning of the highways in its area so far as the cleaning of them appears to the authority to be necessary in the interests of public health or the amenities of the area; but that duty shall not include a duty to undertake the cleaning of any special road which is a trunk road or any other cleaning falling to be done by a highway authority in pursuance of the preceding subsection.

(3) A local authority may, with the consent of any person who has an interest in or is the occupier of any relevant land, arrange for the cleaning of the land and may enter into an agreement with such a person for the payment by him of charges in respect of the cleaning; and in this subsection "relevant land" means any land in the open air to which members of the public have access, either as of right or otherwise, and which is not the site of a highway.

(4) In the preceding provisions of this section and in the following section—

"highway" means highway maintainable at the public expense within the meaning of the Highways Act 1959;

"local authority" means the council of a district or London borough and the Common Council of the City of London; and

"special road" and "trunk road" have the same meanings as in the Highways Act 1959.

(5) [*Applies to Scotland only.*] [**42**]

DEFINITIONS

Amenities:	see note to s. 7 (4)
Highway authority:	see s. 187 of the Local Government Act 1972
Local authority:	sub-s. (4)
Relevant land:	sub-s. (3)
Special road:	sub-s. (4)
Trunk road:	sub-s. (4)

GENERAL NOTE

This section replaces s. 77 of the Public Health Act 1936 (repealed by Sch. 4). Duties are imposed by sub-ss. (1) and (2) on local and highway authorities requiring them to clean highways; the duties are enforceable by means of the default powers of the Secretary of State under section 97. These duties are, however, limited in scope, but they are supplemented by the litter abatement provisions of s. 24.

23. Prohibition of parking to facilitate street cleaning

(1) Where in the case of any part of a highway (hereafter in this section referred to as "the relevant area") the highway authority for the relevant area or the local authority in whose area the relevant area is situated considers that, in order to facilitate the cleaning of the relevant area on a particular day (here-

after in this section referred to as "the relevant day"), it is appropriate to prohibit the parking of vehicles in the relevant area during certain hours of the relevant day, the authority may give notice in accordance with the following provisions of this section prohibiting such parking.

(2) Such a notice must specify the relevant area, the relevant day and the hours in question and must be in such form and contain such other information as are prescribed; and subject to paragraphs (*a*) and (*b*) of the following subsection a copy of the notice must—

(*a*) be served in accordance with regulations on the occupier of any premises adjoining the relevant area and on any prescribed person; and

(*b*) be conspicuously displayed in accordance with regulations at places in the relevant area.

(3) Regulations may provide—

(*a*) that such a notice which is served in a prescribed manner in respect of any premises shall be treated for the purposes of this section as served on the occupier of the premises;

(*b*) that a failure to serve or display a notice as required by virtue of this section apart from the regulations shall in prescribed circumstances be disregarded for the purposes of this section; and

(*c*) for the covering up of traffic signs and parking meters on the relevant day or any part of it, but without prejudice to the effect of the notice in question if regulations made in pursuance of this paragraph are not observed.

(4) Regulations may also provide that sections 20, 52, and 53 of the Road Traffic Regulation Act 1967 (which among other things provide for the removal, storage and disposal of vehicles left on roads in contravention of a statutory prohibition) shall have effect, in relation to any vehicle which is or was standing on any part of a highway while parking on that part is or was prohibited by virtue of this section, with such modifications as are prescribed.

(5) If, either before or during the hours on the relevant day which are specified in a notice given by an authority as mentioned in subsection (1) of this section, the authority displays such further notices in the relevant area and takes such other steps (if any) as are prescribed, the prohibition on parking attributable to the notice so given shall not come into force or, if it is already in force, shall cease to be in force.

(6) It shall be the duty of the highway authority for any part of a highway and of the local authority in whose area the part is situated to co-operate with each other in performing the functions conferred on them by virtue of this section; and where a highway authority or a local authority gives notice as mentioned in subsection (1) of this section in respect of any part of a highway for which it is the highway authority or, as the case may be, which is within its area, any other authority which is the highway authority for that part or which is the local authority within whose area that part is situated shall, with the approval of the authority which gave the notice, be entitled to act in pursuance of this section as if the other authority had given similar notice.

(7) Where any parking in the relevant area is, by virtue of a notice given as mentioned in subsection (1) of this section, prohibited during specified hours on the relevant day, no right of action shall accrue to any person by reason of the fact that all or some of the cleaning of the relevant area which the highway

authority or, as the case may be, the local authority proposes to do or has done during those hours is not cleaning which that authority has or had power to do if the other of those authorities has or had power to do it.

(8) Any reference in the preceding provisions of this section to a part of a highway includes any such part on which the parking of vehicles is, apart from this section, authorised by virtue of any enactment whether on payment or free of charge; and where the parking of vehicles on such a part is prohibited by virtue of this section a person shall not be entitled to recover any sum paid by him in respect of the parking of a vehicle there. **[43]**

DEFINITIONS

Premises:	s. 105 (1)
Prescribed:	by regulations made by the Secretary of State: s. 105 (1)
Relevant area:	see sub-s. (1)

GENERAL NOTE

This section allows a local authority or a highway authority (and although the two must co-operate, either authority *may* act, presumably normally, the collection authority) to prohibit parking of vehicles within a relevant area of highway(s) at certain hours on a particular day (presumably in each week) so as to facilitate the cleaning of the area. Note that the section is *not* designed to facilitate refuse collection from dustbins at houses or other premises.

SUB-S. (2)

The method of service must be as prescribed; service in accordance with s. 233 of the Local Government Act 1972 will not necessarily be sufficient. See also sub-s. (3).

"Adjoining is not a precise word, but must include all premises having access to or fronting on any highway in question. Does an upper floor flat "adjoin" the street?: see *Buckinghamshire County Council* v. *Trigg*, [1963] 1 All E.R. 403.

SUB-S. (4)

If regulations do so provide, vehicles obstructing the street cleansing process may be liable to be removed. There is, however, no provision in this section making it an offence for the driver of a vehicle or other person to disregard a restriction on parking imposed by the section.

24. Litter

(1) It shall be the duty of the council of each county in England and Wales and the local authorities of which the areas are included in the county and, where the county includes land in a National Park, the Park authority to consult from time to time together, and with such voluntary bodies as the council and the authorities consider appropriate and as agree to participate in the consultations, about the steps which the council and each of the authorities and bodies is to take for the purpose of abating litter in the county; and it shall be the duty of the county council—

(*a*) to prepare and from time to time revise a statement of the steps which the council and each of the authorities and bodies agrees to take for that purpose; and

(*b*) to take such steps as in its opinion will give adequate publicity in the county to the statement; and (*c*) to keep a copy of the statement available at its principal office for inspection by the public free of charge at all reasonable hours.

(2) The preceding subsection shall apply to Greater London and the Greater London Council as it applies to a county and the council of a county, and in that subsection "local authority" means a collection authority, a parish council, a parish meeting and a community council and "Park authority" means the National Parks Committee or the joint or special planning board for the Park in question.

(3) [*Applies to Scotland only.*]

(4) The Secretary of State may with the consent of the Treasury make grants to any body for the purpose of assisting the body to encourage the public not to deface places in Great Britain by litter. [**44**]

DEFINITIONS

Collection authority:	s. 30 (1)
Local authority:	sub-s. (2)

GENERAL NOTE

This section requires the preparation of a "litter abatement statement" by a county council, in consultation with other bodies. The Litter Acts 1958 and 1969, making it an offence for a person to deposit litter anywhere in the open air, are not affected by the present Act.

SUB-S. (1)

"Consult with": see note to s. 2 (1).

SUB-S. (4)

These grants may be made to a national organisation, and not only to local authorities.

Supplemental

25. Disposal of waste underground by Coal Board, etc.

(1) Where the Coal Commission or the National Coal Board (hereafter in this section referred to respectively as "the Commission" and "the Board") or any licensees of the Commission or the Board have, in the course of operations carried on for coal-mining purposes, exercised in respect of any underground land a right conferred on the Commission or the Board or the licensees by virtue of section 15 of the Coal Act 1938 (under which the Commission had and the Board have among other things, subject to the restrictions mentioned in that section, the right in the course of such operations to enter and to execute works and do the other acts there mentioned in underground land not vested in them), that section shall have effect in relation to the land as if the reference to coal-mining purposes included the purposes of disposing of waste.

(2) The preceding subsection shall apply to any underground land which—

(*a*) is neither land included in a mine of coal which is vested in the Board nor land to which the said section 15 as modified by the preceding subsection applies apart from this subsection; but

(*b*) is included in the boundaries of a cavity adjacent to such land as is mentioned in the preceding paragraph,

as if the Board had, in the course of such operations as are mentioned in the preceding subsection, exercised such a right as is so mentioned in respect of the underground land.

(3) Paragraph (*e*) of the proviso to the said section 15 (which provides that the Board and its licensees shall not by virtue of that section be entitled to do any act which apart from that section would be actionable as a tresspass or nuisance and likely to cause damage of more than a nominal amount) shall not apply to any right exercisable by virtue of subsection (1) or (2) of this section; but a person having an interest in any underground land who suffers damage by reference to that interest in consequence of the exercise of such a right shall be entitled to recover compensation from the Board in respect of the damage if the amount of the compensation will exceed £50, and any dispute as to a person's entitlement to compensation in pursuance of this subsection or as to the amount of the compensation shall be determined by arbitration.

(4) The Board and any licensees of the Board shall not be entitled by virtue of subsection (1) or (2) of this section to exercise any right in respect of any underground land unless they have, not less than twenty-eight days before exercising the right, published in a local newspaper circulating in the locality in which the land is situated a notice specifying the right and indicating the location of the land and a place in the said locality at which a plan showing the location of the land may be inspected by the public free of charge at all reasonable hours.

(5) Expressions used in this section and Part I of the Coal Act 1938 have the same meanings in this section as in that Part. [**45**]

DEFINITIONS

The Board:	sub-s. (1)
The Commission:	sub-s. (1)
Waste:	s. 30 (1) and see s. 30 (3)

GENERAL NOTE

This section empowers the National Coal Board or its licensees to exercise rights in respect of underground land for coal purposes, to be used for the disposal of waste subject to 28 days advertisement (sub-s. (4)).

26. Outfall pipes for sewage disposal works

(1) Parts V and VI of Schedule 3 to the Water Act 1945 (which relate to the laying of mains and the breaking up of streets) shall apply in relation to outfall pipes and associated works which are provided or to be provided by a water authority for sewage disposal works belonging to the authority as those Parts apply in relation to water mains and pipes but as if in those Parts there were made the modifications specified in paragraphs (*a*) to (*c*) of section 12 (7) of this Act.

(2) This section does not apply to Scotland. [**46**]

27. Interference with refuse tips and dustbins, etc.

(1) No person shall sort over or disturb—

(*a*) anything deposited at a place provided by a disposal authority or a collection authority for the deposit of waste or in a receptacle for waste which is provided by such an authority or a parish or community council for public use; or

(*b*) the contents of any receptacle for waste which, in accordance with regulations made by virtue of section 13 (7) of this Act, is placed on any highway or in any other place with a view to its being emptied,

unless he is authorised to do so by the authority or council in the case of anything deposited as mentioned in paragraph (*a*) above or, in the case of such a receptacle as is mentioned in paragraph (*b*) above, unless he is a person entitled to the custody of the receptacle or is authorised to do so by such a person or is a person having the function of emptying the receptacle.

. . . . .

(2) A person who contravenes any of the provisions of the preceding subsection shall be guilty of an offence and liable on summary conviction to a fine of an amount not exceeding £100. **[47]**

DEFINITIONS

Collection authority:	s. 30 (1)
Disposal authority:	s. 30 (1)
Receptacle for waste:	see s. 13 (8)
Waste:	s. 30 (1), and see s. 30 (3)

GENERAL NOTE

This section replaces s. 76 (2) of the Public Health Act 1936 (repealed by Sch. 4). Section 156, *ibid.*, making it an offence to place or cause to be placed in any dustbin or ashpit, any matter which it is known has been exposed to infection from a notifiable disease, is left unrepealed. Under the Explosives Act 1875 an order has been made (S.R. & O. 1924, No. 1129) making it an offence to place explosives in any receptacle or place appropriated for refuse.

28. Supplementary provisions relating to pipes

(1) Where an authority provides pipes in pursuance of section 12 (6), 14 (5), 15 (2), 21 (4) or 26 of this Act, it shall be the duty of the authority—

(*a*) except where the authority is a collection authority and the pipes are situated in its area, to send to the collection authority in whose area the pipes are situated a map in the prescribed form showing the location of the pipes; and

(*b*) where the authority is a collection authority and the pipes are situated in its area, to prepare such a map;

and it shall be the duty of an authority by which a map is received in pursuance of paragraph (*a*) of this subsection or is prepared in pursuance of paragraph (*b*) of this subsection to secure that a copy of the map is available at its principal offices for inspection by the public free of charge at all reasonable hours.

. . . . .

(2) Section 25 of the Public Health Act 1936 (under which the erection of buildings over a sewer or drain may be prevented or controlled by a local authority or, on appeal, by a magistrates' court) shall have effect as if references to a drain included any pipe provided as mentioned in the preceding subsection and as if the reference to the map of sewers required by that Act to be kept deposited at the offices of an authority included any map required by the preceding subsection to be kept available at the offices of the authority.

(3) [*Applies to Scotland only.*]

(4) References to pipes in the preceding provisions of this section include associated works. **[48]**

DEFINITION

Collection authority: s. 30 (1)

SUB-S. (2)

Section 25 of the Public Health Act 1936 applies only when plans are required to be deposited under the Building Regulations 1972. As to sewer maps, see s. 32 of the 1936 Act.

29. Modification of Parts I and II to avoid duplication of control

The Secretary of State may by regulations make such modifications of this Part of this Act and Part II of this Act as he considers appropriate with a view to securing that the provisions of one but not both of those Parts apply to prescribed acts and omissions. [**49**]

30. Interpretation etc. of Part I

(1) Subject to the following subsection, in this Part of this Act—

"associated works", in relation to pipes, means any of the following connected with the pipes, namely, any valve, filter, stopcock, pump, inspection chamber and manhole and such other works as are prescribed;

"collection authority" means the council of a district or a London borough, the Common Council of the City of London, the Sub-Treasurer of the Inner Temple and the Under Treasurer of the Middle Temple and "English collection authority" means a collection authority of which the area is in England;

"controlled waste" means household, industrial and commercial waste or any such waste;

"disposal authority" means the council of a county in England, the council of a district in Wales and the Greater London Council, "English disposal authority" means a disposal authority of which the area is in England and "relevant disposal authority", in relation to an English collection authority, means the disposal authority of which the area includes that of the collection authority;

"disposal licence" has the meaning assigned to it by section 3 (1) of this Act, and "holder" in relation to such a licence shall be construed in accordance with section 8 (3) of this Act;

"private dwelling" means—

(*a*) a hereditament or premises used wholly for the purposes of a private dwelling or private dwellings as determined in accordance with Schedule 13 to the General Rate Act 1967; and

(*b*) a caravan as defined in section 29 (1) of the Caravan Sites and Control of Development Act 1960 (disregarding the amendment made by section 13 (2) of the Caravan Sites Act 1968) which usually and for the time being is situated on a caravan site within the meaning of that Act;

"relevant land" means—

(*a*) in relation to a proposal to issue a disposal licence, the land on which activities may be carried on in pursuance of the licence if it is issued in accordance with the proposal; and

(*b*) in relation to a disposal licence, the land on which activities may be carried on in pursuance of the licence, and references to land in the preceding paragraphs include such water as is mentioned in section 4 (4) of this Act;

"waste" includes—

(*a*) any substance which constitutes a scrap material or an effluent or other unwanted surplus substance arising from the application of any process; and

(*b*) any substance or article which requires to be disposed of as being broken, worn out, contaminated or otherwise spoiled,

but does not include a substance which is an explosive within the meaning of the Explosives Act 1875;

and for the purposes of this Part of this Act any thing which is discarded or otherwise dealt with as if it were waste shall be presumed to be waste unless the contrary is proved.

(2) [*Applies to Scotland only.*]

(3) Subject to the following subsection, for the purposes of this Part of this Act—

(*a*) household waste consists of waste from a private dwelling or residential home or from premises forming part of a university of school or other educational establishment or forming part of a hospital or nursing home;

(*b*) industrial waste consists of waste from any factory within the meaning of the Factories Act 1961 and any premises occupied by a body corporate established by or under any enactment for the purpose of carrying on under national ownership any industry or part of an industry or any undertaking, excluding waste from any mine or quarry; and

(*c*) commercial waste consists of waste from premises used wholly or mainly for the purposes of a trade or business or the purposes of sport, recreation or entertainment excluding—

(i) household and industrial waste, and

(ii) waste from any mine or quarry and waste from premises used for agriculture within the meaning of the Agriculture Act 1947, or, in Scotland, the Agriculture (Scotland) Act 1948, and

(iii) waste of any other description prescribed for the purposes of this sub-paragraph.

(4) Regulations may provide that waste of a prescribed description shall be treated for the purposes of prescribed provisions of this Part of this Act as being or not being household waste or industrial waste or commercial waste; but no regulations shall be made by virtue of the preceding provisions of this subsection in respect of such waste as is mentioned in paragraph (*c*) (ii) of the preceding subsection and references in those provisions and in the preceding subsection to waste do not include sewage except so far as regulations provide otherwise.

In this subsection "sewage" includes matter in or from a privy within the meaning of section 12 (5) of this Act.

(5) Except as provided by regulations made by virtue of this subsection, nothing in this Part of this Act applies to radioactive waste within the meaning of the Radioactive Substances Act 1960; but regulations may—

(*a*) provide for prescribed provisions of this Part of this Act to have effect with such modifications as the Secretary of State considers appropriate for the purposes of dealing with such radioactive waste;

(*b*) make such modifications of the said Act of 1960 and any other Act as the Secretary of State considers appropriate in consequence of the passing of this Part of this Act or in connection with regulations made by virtue of the preceding paragraph. [**50**]

SUB-S. (1)

General Rate Act 1967, Sch. 13. This schedule includes elaborate provisions for the determination of whether premises are used for the purposes of a private dwelling or dwellings. In particular it deals with cases where a hereditament is used for the letting of rooms; if it consists mainly of land used as a site for moveable dwellings, it cannot be classed as a private dwelling.

Caravan Sites and Control of Development Act 1960: "caravan" in this section is defined to mean a moveable structure designed or adapted for human habitation, not including a tent. Presumably the amendment dealing with twin-unit caravans in s. 13 of the Caravan Sites Act 1968 is not considered relevant for present purposes. A "caravan site" is defined by s. 1 (4) of the Act of 1960 to mean "land on which a caravan is stationed for the purposes of human habitation and land which is used in conjunction with land on which a caravan is so stationed."

SUB-S. (2)

As to explosives in dustbins, see note to s. 27.

SUB-S. (3)

But these definitions may be altered by regulations made under sub-s. (4).

SUB-S. (5)

"Radioactive waste": is defined in s. 18 (4) of the Act of 1960, and "waste" is in turn, for the purposes of that Act, defined in s. 19 (1). The stringent controls imposed by that Act over radioactive substances are virtually unaffected by the present statute, except for the increases in penalties provided for in s. 99 and Sch. 2. This subsection applies also to Part II of the Act: see s. 56 (6).

PART II

POLLUTION OF WATER

INTRODUCTION TO PART II

[**51**] This Part is concerned with the prevention of pollution of *water*—inland, coastal and underground, as the legislation makes a departure from the "rivers and streams" of the Rivers (Prevention of Pollution) Acts 1876, 1951 and 1961. The 1951 Act is repealed *in toto* (Sch. 4) and so is almost the whole of the 1961 Act. It leaves almost unaffected (but see Sch. 4) the Salmon and Freshwater Fisheries Act 1923. In general, Part II applies to "relevant waters", which is defined by s. 31 (1) to mean collectively any "stream" (itself defined in s. 56 (1), and s. 56 (3), to include any river or inland water except lakes, etc., other than those prescribed, sewers and tidal waters), any "controlled waters" (coastal waters within a three nautical mile limit: *ibid.*) and any underground water specified in prescribed documents (*ibid.*). Section 31 makes it an offence (replacing s. 1 of the 1951 Act) for any person to cause or knowingly permit poisonous, noxious or polluting matter to enter relevant waters, subject to certain detailed defences (see sub-s. (2)). One of these defences is to the effect that the discharge was made pursuant to a disposal

licence given under Part I, or pursuant to a consent given by the water authority or the Secretary of State under Part II; another is that the discharge was in accordance with "good agricultural practice" (but this may be restricted by a notice served by the Secretary of State under s. 51).

[**52**] Under s. 31 (4) regulations may be made by the Secretary of State to require precautions to be taken to avoid pollution of water, and under s. 31 (5) he may prescribe areas where special precautions may be required.

[**53**] Section 32 controls the discharge into relevant waters or the sea outside controlled waters by means of a pipe from the land, of any trade or sewage effluent, unless the consent of the water authority has first been obtained. Under s. 33 a water authority may control another common source of pollution by making byelaws regulating the keeping or use of vessels provided with prescribed sanitary appliances on a stream or "restricted waters" (see s. 56 (1)). After 1978 it is the intention that such vessels shall be completely banned from all "streams" (see s. 33 (2), although vessels equipped with self-contained chemical closets would be permitted. Where such byelaws have been made, the water authority will be under a duty to collect and dispose of waste from vessels in their area, under s. 47.

[**54**] Sections 34–42 are concerned with consents to discharges. Applications for consent are to be made to the water authority, and consent may be refused or granted unconditionally, or granted subject to any reasonable conditions and in particular subject to those of a kind specified in s. 34 (4). Certain applications for consent must by direction of the Secretary of State, be referred to him for determination, and in such a case he may if he thinks fit hold a local inquiry (s. 35). Section 36 provides for publication of applications for consent (subject to exemptions in special cases under s. 32) while s. 37 allows a water authority to revoke an existing consent or to alter or impose conditions, subject to restrictions imposed by s. 38. Appeals against refusals or revocation of consent, or of conditions attached to a consent, lie to the Secretary of State under s. 39. On any such appeal the Secretary of State may *ex proprio motu*, or on the direction of the High Court shall, state a case for the opinion of the High Court on a question of law arising in those proceedings (s. 39 (8)). Section 40 contains transitional provisions relating to consents, and water authorities are required to maintain registers of applications for consent, in accordance with regulations to be made by the Secretary of State showing how the applications have been determined (s. 41). It should be noted that a provision in the original Bill whereby an action for an injunction to prevent a discharge of polluting matter into a stream, at the instance of a riparian owner, would not be possible if the discharge had become the subject of a consent given by the water authority, has been dropped and mercifully does not appear in the Act.

[**55**] The controls over the discharge of trade effluent into public sewers, contained in the Public Health (Drainage of Trade Effluent) Act 1937 and the Public Health Act 1961, and administered since 1st April 1974 (under the Water Act 1973) by the water authorities, remain on the statute book, but are extended by ss. 43 and 44. In future all discharges of trade effluent (as defined in s. 105) will be subject to control, as the former exemptions for pre-1937 discharges are now withdrawn. Conditions (in particular as to charges) subject to which these discharges have been permitted may in future be varied before the lapse of the period of two years specified in s. 60 of the Public Health Act 1961 if the water authority consider this necessary in order to provide proper protection for persons likely to be affected by discharges (see s. 45).

[**56**] Section 41 is an important new provision, in that it requires water authorities to take action to forestall pollution of water and to remedy the effects of injurious pollution (i.e. pollution injurious to the fauna or flora of the stream: s. 46 (8)).

[**57**] Section 48 empowers a water authority to make byelaws excluding un-

registered vessels from streams in their area, and s. 49 makes it an offence for any person to cause a deposit to be carried away in suspension in the water of a stream, or to cut or uproot any substantial amount of vegetation into a stream. Under s. 52 the Secretary of State may provide for charges to be made in respect of consents to the discharge of trade or sewage effluent. Regulations may be made under s. 55 dealing with a water authority's own discharges.

[**58**] Finance: The financing of the administration of Part II is not without difficulty. Under the Water Act 1973, water authorities have powers to charge for "facilities" (a word usually widely construed, see Public Health Act 1936, s. 271) provided by them, e.g. in making connections with water supply and sewerage. The powers of the former river authorities to levy precepts on local authorities under the Water Resources Act 1963, have been repealed by the Water Act 1973 (Sch. 8), and the administration of the prevention of pollution of water provisions of the present Act has not been expressly provided for. It would be difficult to describe some of these services as amounting to the "provision of facilities". Their costs may, however, be included in the sums to be collected by rating authorities as general services: see the Water Authorities (Collection of Charges) Order 1974 (S.I. 1974 No. 445).

[**59**] Land Acquisiton: The powers to acquire land conferred on the former river authorities by the Water Resources Act 1963, are however kept alive by the Water Act 1973, for the benefit of the water authorities, and these could be used for the purposes of administering Part II of the present Act (see Water Resources Act 1963, ss. 65 and 67, and Water Act 1973, s. 9). Water authorities also have the compulsory acquisition powers given by s. 306 of the Public Health Act 1936 (formerly repealed by the Local Government Act 1972, but restored to this extent by Art. 27 of Sch. 3 to the present Act).

Control of entry of polluting matter and effluents into water

31. Control of pollution of rivers and coastal waters, etc.

(1) Subject to subsections (2) and (3) of this section, a person shall be guilty of an offence if he causes or knowingly permits—

(*a*) any poisonous, noxious or polluting matter to enter any stream or controlled waters or any specified underground water (hereafter in this Part of this Act referred to collectively as "relevant waters"); or

(*b*) any matter to enter a stream so as to tend (either directly or in combination with other matter which he or another person causes or permits to enter the stream) to impede the proper flow of the water of the stream in a manner leading or likely to lead to a substantial aggravation of pollution due to other causes or of the consequences of such pollution; or

(*c*) any solid waste matter to enter a stream or restricted waters.

(2) A person shall not be guilty of an offence by virtue of the preceding subsection if—

(*a*) the entry in question is authorised by, or is a consequence of an act authorised by, a disposal licence or a consent given by the Secretary of State or a water authority in pursuance of this Act and the entry or act is in accordance with the conditions, if any, to which the licence or consent is subject; or

(*b*) the entry in question is authorised by, or is a consequence of an act authorised by—

(i) section 34 of the Water Act 1945 or, in Scotland, section 50 of the Water (Scotland) Act 1946 (which among other things relate to temporary discharges by water undertakers and corresponding Scottish authorities in connection with the construction of works) or any prescribed enactment, or

(ii) any provision of a local Act or statutory order which expressly confers power to discharge effluent into water, or

(iii) any licence granted under the Dumping at Sea Act 1974; or

(*c*) the entry in question is attributable to an act or omission which is in accordance with good agricultural practice other than an act or omission which—

(i) is of a kind specified in a notice which is in force when the entry occurs and which was served in pursuance of subsection (3) (*a*) of section 51 of this Act on the occupier or any previous occupier of the place where the act or omission occurs, and

(ii) occurs after the expiration of the period of twenty-eight days beginning with the date entered in the register mentioned in subsection (4) of that section as the date of service of the notice; or

(*d*) the entry in question is caused or permitted in an emergency in order to avoid danger to the public and, as soon as reasonably practicable after the entry occurs, particulars of the entry are furnished to the water authority in whose area it occurs; or

(*e*) the matter in question is trade or sewage effluent discharged as mentioned in paragraph (*a*) of subsection (1) of the following section or matter discharged as mentioned in paragraph (*b*) or (*c*) of that subsection and the entry in question is not from a vessel;

and a person shall not be guilty of an offence by virtue of the preceding subsection by reason only of his permitting water from an abandoned mine to enter relevant waters.

(3) A person shall not by virtue of paragraph (*b*) or (*c*) of subsection (1) of this section be guilty of an offence by reason of his depositing the solid refuse of a mine or quarry on any land so that it falls or is carried into a stream or restricted waters if—

(*a*) he deposits the refuse on the land with the consent (which shall not be unreasonably withheld) of the water authority in whose area the land is situated; and

(*b*) no other site for the deposit is reasonably practicable; and

(*c*) he takes all reasonably practicable steps to prevent the refuse from entering the stream or restricted waters.

(4) Provision may be made by regulations as to the precautions to be taken, by any person having the custody or control of any poisonous, noxious or polluting matter, for the purpose of preventing the matter from entering any relevant waters; and the regulations may provide that a contravention of the regulations shall be an offence and may prescribe the maximum penalty for the offence.

(5) Where it appears to the Secretary of State that, with a view to preventing poisonous, noxious or polluting matter from entering any relevant waters, it is appropriate to prohibit or restrict the carrying on in a particular area of activities which he considers are likely to result in pollution of the waters, then, subject to section 104 (3) of this Act, he may by regulations—

(*a*) designate that area; and

(*b*) provide that prescribed activities shall not be carried on at any place within the area except with the consent (which shall not be unreasonably withheld) of the water authority in whose area the place is situated and in accordance with any reasonable conditions to which the consent is subject; and

(*c*) provide that a contravention of the regulations shall be an offence and prescribe the maximum penalty for the offence.

(6) A water authority may by byelaws make such provision as the authority considers appropriate for prohibiting or regulating the washing or cleaning, in any stream or controlled waters in its area, of things of a kind specified in the byelaws; and a person who contravenes any byelaws made by virtue of this subsection shall be guilty of an offence and liable on summary conviction to a fine not exceeding £200 or such smaller sum as is specified in the byelaws.

(7) A person guilty of an offence by virtue of paragraph (*a*) or (*b*) of subsection (1) of this section shall be liable—

(*a*) on summary conviction, to imprisonment for a term not exceeding three months or a fine not exceeding £400 or both;

(*b*) on conviction on indictment, to imprisonment for a term not exceeding two years or a fine or both;

and a person guilty of an offence by virtue of paragraph (*c*) of that subsection shall be liable on summary conviction to a fine not exceeding £200.

(8) The maximum penalties prescribed in pursuance of subsections (4) and (5) of this section shall not exceed the penalties specified in paragraphs (*a*) and (*b*) of the preceding subsection and, in the case of a continuing offence punishable on summary conviction, £50 for each day on which the offence continues after conviction for the offence.

(9) In subsection (2) of this section—

"disposal licence" has the same meaning as in Part I of this Act;

"local Act" includes enactments in a public general Act which amend a local Act;

"statutory order" means an order, byelaw, scheme or award made under an Act of Parliament, including an order or scheme confirmed by Parliament or brought into operation in accordance with special parliamentary procedure;

and for the purposes of paragraph (*c*) of that subsection any practice recommended in a code approved for the purposes of that paragraph by the Minister of Agriculture, Fisheries and Food or, in Scotland, by the Secretary of State shall, without prejudice to any evidence that any further practice is good agricultural practice, be deemed to be good agricultural practice. [**60**]

DEFINITIONS

Controlled waters:	s. 56 (1)
Disposal licence:	s. 3 (1), applied by sub-s. (9) of this section
Local Act:	see sub-s. (9)
Regulations:	made by the Secretary of State under s. 104: s. 105 (1)
Sewage effluent:	s. 56 (1)
Specified underground water:	s. 56 (1)
Stream:	s. 56 (1) and s. 56 (3)
Trade effluent:	s. 105 (1)
Vessel:	s. 105 (1)
Water authority:	Water Act 1973, s. 2

GENERAL NOTE

This important section replaces s. 2 of the Rivers (Prevention of Pollution) Act 1951 (repealed *in toto* by Sch. 4) but it makes provision as well as for the substantive offence of polluting a stream, and a number of special defences, such as that the entry in question was in accordance with "good agricultural practice" (as to which see sub-s. (9)) or that it was due to an emergency so as to avoid danger to the public. Special provision is made for the deposit of solid refuse from a mine or quarry (sub-s. (3)).

Summary proceedings for an offence under s. 31 (1), or for a contravention of regulations made under s. 31 (4) or (5), or for a contravention of byelaws made under s. 31 (6), may be brought within one year from the commission of the offence: s. 87 (3).

SUB-S. (1)

For the first time in legislation, this offence extends to underground water, but even now it applies only to *specified* water (see s. 56 (1)). "Controlled waters" include the sea within the three mile limit and estuaries round the coast of Britain. For comment on "poisonous, noxious or polluting", see note to s. 3 (3). The former special exemption for the discharge of innocuous colouring matter (1951 Act, s. 11 (3)) has not been repeated in the present Act. "Causes or knowingly permits": a defendant does not "cause" an effluent to enter a stream if a third party interferes with plant or equipment: *Impress* (*Worcester*), *Ltd*. v. *Rees*, [1971] 2 All E.R. 357. On the other hand a defendant may be liable under the present section if effluent escapes inadvertently and in the absence of any negligence on the part of the defendant or his employees, as a result of natural causes: see *Alphacell* v. *Woodward*, [1972] A.C. 824; [1972] 2 All E.R. 475. Special defences are, however, afforded by sub-s. (2). Paragraph (*b*) is concerned only with the discharge of matter which is liable to impede the flow of water, and not with pollution. It may not always be clear as to who may be liable if A discharges an effluent innocuous in itself, and B discharges another equally innocuous effluent, but because of the chemical or other reaction of the two effluents, pollution of the stream is caused. In most cases such a case would be caught by s. 31. For penalties for an offence under this subsection, see sub-ss. (7) and (8). It will be noted that para. (*c*) applies to *any* solid waste, whether or not it is noxious or polluting.

SUB-S. (2)

As to consents for discharges, see s. 34. The Secretary of State may by regulations add to the enactments which afford a defence in proceedings under this section.

The Dumping at Sea Act 1974 prohibits the dumping of substances or articles in United Kingdom waters, or from a British ship or aircraft, elsewhere at sea, except pursuant to a licence issued by the Minister of Agriculture, Fisheries and Food, or the Secretary of State for Scotland.

Certain conditions may be disregarded for this purpose: see s. 36 (8). As to what is good agricultural practice, see sub-s. (8). Particular practices may be prevented by a notice served by the Secretary of State on the application of the water authority under s. 51. In a case of emergency particulars of any entry to relevant waters must be furnished to the water authority; the Act does not specifically require the particulars to be furnished in writing, but it is obviously desirable that this should be so, and service should then be affected in accordance with s. 95.

SUB-S. (3)

"Mine" and "quarry" are to be understood as defined in the Mines and Quarries Act 1954: s. 105 (1). "Reasonably practicable" is not defined for the present purpose, but it was explained by ASQUITH, L.J. (when considering its use in a similar statutory context) as being—"a narrower term than 'physically possible' and seems to me to imply that a computation must be made by the owner in which the *quantum* of risk is placed on one scale and the sacrifice involved in the measures necessary for averting the risk (whether in money, time or trouble) is placed in the other; and that if it be shown that there is a gross disproportion between them—the risk being insignificant in relation to the sacrifice—the defendants discharge the onus on them. Moreover, this computation falls to be made by the owner at a point of time anterior to the accident:" *Edwards* v. *National Coal Board* [1949] 1 K.B. 704, at p. 712. But in relation to Part III, see s. 72.

SUB-S. (5)

Special preliminary procedure has to be followed before regulations are made under this subsection: s. 104 (3). See also s. 39 (7)

SUB-S. (6)

Water authority byelaws need to be confirmed by the Secretary of State under s. 36 (3) and Sch. 7, Part II of the Water Act 1973, before they come into effect.

SUB-S. (9)

The code referred to at the end of this subsection may be made in any form, and although virtually (if not in fact) subordinate legislation, does not have to be made by way of statutory instrument.

32. Control of discharges of trade and sewage effluent, etc., into rivers and coastal waters, etc.

(1) Subject to subsections (3) to (5) of this section, a person shall be guilty of an offence if he causes or knowingly permits—

(*a*) any trade effluent or sewage effluent to be discharged—

(i) into any relevant waters, or

(ii) from land in Great Britain through a pipe into the sea outside controlled waters, or

(iii) from a building or from plant on to or into any land or into any lake, loch or pond which does not discharge into a stream; or

(*b*) any matter other than trade or sewage effluent to be discharged into relevant waters from a sewer as defined by section 343 of the Public Health Act 1936, or, in Scotland, by section 59 (1) of the Sewerage (Scotland) Act 1968 or from a drain as so defined; or

(*c*) any matter other than trade or sewage effluent to be discharged into relevant waters from a drain which a highway authority or other person is entitled to keep open by virtue of section 103 of the Highways Act 1959, or in Scotland from works which a highway authority is obliged or entitled to keep open by virtue of section 10 of the Roads (Scotland) Act 1970, and in respect of which the water authority in whose area the discharge occurs has, not later than the beginning of the period of three months ending with the date of the discharge, served on the highway authority or other person a notice stating that this paragraph is to apply to the drain or works, unless the discharge is made with the consent in pursuance of section 34 of this Act of the water authority in whose area the discharge occurs (or, in a case falling within paragraph (*a*) (ii) of this subsection, of the water authority whose area includes the point at which the pipe passes or first passes into or under controlled waters from the sea outside them) and is in accordance with the conditions, if any, to which the consent is subject.

(2) Where any sewage effluent is discharged as mentioned in paragraph (*a*) of the preceding subsection from any works or sewer vested in a water authority and the authority did not cause or knowingly permit the discharge but was bound to receive into the works or sewer, either unconditionally or subject to conditions which were observed, matter included in the discharge, the authority shall be deemed for the purposes of that subsection to have caused the discharge.

(3) The Secretary of State may—

(*a*) by an order made before subsection (1) of this section comes into force provide that that subsection shall not, while the order is in force, apply to discharges which are of a kind or in an area specified in the order and for which, if this Act had not been passed, consent in pursuance of the Rivers (Prevention of Pollution) Acts 1951 to 1961 or the Rivers (Prevention of Pollution) (Scotland) Acts 1951 and 1965 or section 72 of the Water Resources Act 1963 would not have been required;

(*b*) by order vary or revoke any order in force by virtue of the preceding paragraph;

and an order made by virtue of this subsection may require any water authority specified in the order to publish in a manner so specified such information about the order as is so specified.

(4) Subsection (1) of this section shall not apply to any discharge which—

(*a*) is from a vessel; or

(*b*) is authorised by a licence granted under the Dumping at Sea Act 1974; or

(*c*) is caused or permitted in an emergency in order to avoid danger to the public if, as soon as reasonably practicable after the discharge occurs, particulars of the discharge are furnished to the water authority in whose area it occurs.

(5) A water authority shall not be guilty of an offence by virtue of subsection (1) of this section by reason only of the fact that a discharge from a sewer or works vested in the authority contravenes conditions of a consent relating to the discharge if—

(*a*) the contravention is attributable to a discharge which another person caused or permitted to be made into the sewer or works; and

(*b*) the authority either was not bound to receive the discharge into the sewer or works or was bound to receive it there subject to conditions but the conditions were not observed; and

(*c*) the authority could not reasonably have been expected to prevent the discharge into the sewer or works;

and a person shall not be guilty of such an offence in consequence of a discharge which he caused or permitted to be made into a sewer or works vested in a water authority if the authority was bound to receive the discharge there either unconditionally or subject to conditions which were observed.

(6) [*Applies to Scotland only.*]

(7) A person who is guilty of an offence by virtue of subsection (1) of this section shall be liable on summary conviction to imprisonment for a term not exceeding three months or a fine not exceeding £400 or both or on conviction on indictment to imprisonment for a term not exceeding two years or a fine or both. **[61]**

DEFINITIONS

Cause or knowingly permit:	see note to s. 31 (1)
Controlled waters:	s. 56 (1)
Relevant waters:	s. 31 (1) (*a*)
Sewage effluent:	s. 56 (1)
Stream:	s. 56 (1)
Trade effluent:	s. 105 (1)
Vessel:	s. 105 (1)
Water authority:	Water Act 1973, s. 2

GENERAL NOTE

This section is a considerable extension on the controls contained in the earlier legislation. In particular it prohibits the discharge of sewage or trade effluent into rivers, estuaries or coastal waters except in accordance with a consent under this Part from the water authority or the Secretary of State. There is, however, a special defence for water authorities (see sub-s. (5)), and it should be remembered that, under the Water Act 1973, all public sewers are now vested in them.

SUB-S. (1)

The definition of "sewer" in s. 343 (1) of the Public Health Act 1936 is not exactly informative, but it does not include a drain as so defined. A "drain" means one used for the drainage of one building or of any buildings or yards appurtenant to buildings within the same curtilage (*ibid.*). We are therefore thrown back to the ordinary "dictionary" meaning of these two words. A sewer may thus be described as a large drain, whether natural or artificial, and whether above or below ground, used for the carrying off from Point A to Point B of surface water, sewage, faecal or other waste matter. It is at least clear that sub-para. (*b*) is not confined to *public* sewers (Public Health Act 1936, s. 20 (as amended)). Section 103 of the Highways Act 1959, as amended by s. 22 of the Highways Act 1971, empowers a highway authority to "keep open" drains constructed or laid for the purpose of draining their highway or otherwise preventing surface water from flowing on to it. Certain conditions may be disregarded for the purposes of this subsection: see s. 36 (8).

SUB-S. (2)

All public sewers and sewage disposal works vest in the water authority by virtue of s. 20 of the Public Health Act 1936, as amended by the Water Act 1973 (see Sch. 8, para. 33 thereof).

SUB-S. (3)

Any such order must be made by statutory instrument: see s. 104 (1).

SUB-S. (4)

Dumping at Sea Act 1974: see note to s. 31 (2). "Reasonably practicable": see note to s. 31 (3).

33. Control of sanitary appliances on vessels

(1) A water authority may by byelaws make such provision as the authority considers appropriate for prohibiting or regulating the keeping or use, on a stream or restricted waters in the area of the authority, of vessels of a kind specified in the byelaws which are provided with sanitary appliances; and a person who contravenes any byelaw made by virtue of this section shall be guilty of an offence.

(2) The Secretary of State may by order provide that any byelaws specified in the order which were made by virtue of section 5 (1) (*c*) of the Rivers (Prevention of Pollution) Act 1951 (which, as extended in pursuance of section 6 of that Act, relates to the keeping on streams and other waters of vessels provided with sanitary appliances) or of section 25 (1) (*c*) of the Rivers (Prevention of Pollution) (Scotland) Act 1951 (which makes corresponding provision with respect to streams in Scotland) shall have effect, with such modifications (if any) as are so specified, as if made by virtue of the preceding subsection.

(3) A person who, after the end of the year 1978, keeps or uses on a stream any vessel provided with a sanitary appliance shall, subject to subsection (8) of this section, be guilty of an offence; and at the end of that year the words "a stream or" in subsection (1) of this section shall cease to have effect.

(4) The Secretary of State and the Minister of Agriculture, Fisheries and Food acting jointly or, in relation to Scotland, the Secretary of State may, by an order made after the end of the year 1978 on the application of a water authority or harbour authority, provide that a person who keeps or uses, on any restricted waters in the area of the authority which are specified in the order, any vessel provided with a sanitary appliance shall, subject to subsection (8) of this section, be guilty of an offence; and when an order is in force by virtue of the preceding provisions of this subsection in relation to any restricted waters, then—

(*a*) subsection (1) of this section shall not apply in relation to the waters; and

(*b*) the said Ministers acting jointly or, in relation to Scotland, the Secretary of State may, on the application of or after giving notice to the authority on whose application the order was made, by order revoke the order.

(5) The said Ministers acting jointly or, in relation to Scotland, the Secretary of State may—

(*a*) by order provide that so much of any stream as is specified in the order shall be disregarded for the purposes of subsection (3) of this section and treated as restricted waters for the purposes of the preceding subsection; and

(*b*) by order revoke or vary any order in force by virtue of the preceding paragraph.

(6) In relation to England and Wales paragraphs 1 to 6 of Schedule 8 to the Water Resources Act 1963 (which among other things provide for the publication of a draft of an order to authorise the execution of works, the gazetting of notices relating to the draft order, the furnishing of copies of the draft, the making of an order in the terms of the draft or in those terms with alterations and the making and consideration of objections relating to the draft or alterations) shall have effect in relation to an application for an order in pursuance of subsection (4) of this section (except subsection (4) (*b*)) as those paragraphs have effect in

relation to an application for such an order as is mentioned in the said paragraph 1 but with the substitution—

(*a*) for any reference to the Secretary of State of a reference to him and the Minister of Agriculture, Fisheries and Food acting jointly;

(*b*) for any reference to a water authority of a reference to a harbour authority in a case where the application in question is made by a harbour authority;

(*c*) for any reference to the locality where the operations are to be carried out of a reference to the area of the applicant;

(*d*) for any reference to a period of twenty-eight or twenty-five days of a reference to a period of six weeks; and

(*e*) for the words from "engineering" onwards in paragraph 2 (*a*) of the words "waters specified in the draft are situated",

and as if paragraph 2 (*b*) were omitted.

(7) [*Applies to Scotland only.*]

(8) At and after the end of the year 1978 it shall be the duty of each water authority to make arrangements for the fixing, at the request of a person in charge of a vessel provided with a sanitary appliance, of a seal to the vessel or appliance in such a manner that while the seal is affixed matter cannot pass from the appliance into the water on which the vessel is for the time being situated; and while a seal is affixed to a vessel or appliance in pursuance of the arrangements, the appliance to which the seal relates shall be disregarded for the purposes of subsections (3) and (4) of this section.

(9) Provision may be made by regulations for requiring a person who in prescribed circumstances hires out for payment to another person any vessel provided with a sanitary appliance to give to the other person notice in a prescribed form of prescribed provisions made by or under this section; and a person who fails to comply with a requirement imposed on him by virtue of this subsection shall be guilty of an offence.

(10) In this section—

"harbour authority" has the meaning assigned to it by section 57 (1) of the Harbours Act 1964; and

"sanitary appliance" means a water closet or other prescribed appliance (except a sink, a bath and a shower-bath) which is designed to permit polluting matter to pass into the water on which the vessel in question is for the time being situated;

and a port health authority shall have power to make such arrangements with a water authority as are mentioned in subsection (8) of this section.

(11) A person guilty of an offence by virtue of any of the preceding provisions of this section shall be liable on summary conviction to a fine of an amount not exceeding £200. [**62**]

DEFINITIONS

Controlled waters:	s. 56 (1)
Harbour authority:	sub-s. (10)
Offence:	see sub-s. (11)
Regulations:	made by the Secretary of State: s. 105 (1)
Restricted waters:	s. 56 (1)
Sanitary appliance:	sub-s. (10)
Stream:	s. 56 (1) and s. 56 (3)
Water authority:	Water Act 1973, s. 2

GENERAL NOTE

This section is designed to control the use of inland waters by any vessel provided with a water closet or other appliance, other than sinks and baths, designed to permit polluting matter to pass into the water. It replaces the more restricted power to make byelaws under s. 5 (1) (*c*) of the Rivers (Prevention of Pollution) Act 1951. Water authorities may make byelaws controlling such vessels, and after 1978 the use of any stream by such a vessel will be totally prohibited (sub-s. (3)). The Secretary of State will be able after 1978, by an order made according to a special procedure, to prohibit the use of designated controlled waters or other areas by such vessels. Where the water authority consider that it is necessary to collect waste from vessels in their area as a consequence of the provisions of this section, they will have a duty to do so, and also to arrange for facilities for the washing out of appliances: s. 47. The authority may also exclude unregistered vessels from their area by byelaws made under s. 48.

SUB-S. (1)

Byelaws must be made, and are subject to confirmation by, the Secretary of State, according to s. 36 (3) and Sch. 7, Part II of the Water Act 1973.

SUB-S. (2)

As to sealing of vessels, see sub-s. (7).

SUB-S. (4)

For the procedure regulating the making of such an order, see sub-s. (5), and see also s. 104 (1).

SUB-S. (9)

"Prescribed": by regulations, see s. 105 (1).

SUB-S. (10)

"Harbour authority" is defined in s. 57 (1) of the 1964 Act to mean any person in whom are vested the powers or duties of improving, maintaining or managing a harbour; and "harbour" is widely defined so as to include natural and artificial harbours, ports, havens, estuaries, etc.

Consents for discharges

34. Consents for discharges of trade and sewage effluent, etc.

(1) An application to a water authority for consent in pursuance of this section for discharges of any effluent or other matter shall state—

(*a*) the place at which it is proposed to make the discharges to which the application relates;

(*b*) the nature and composition of the matter proposed to be discharged and the maximum temperature of it at the time when it is proposed to be discharged;

(*c*) the maximum quantity of the matter which it is proposed to discharge on any one day and the highest rate at which it is proposed to discharge it;

and a water authority may if it thinks fit treat an application for consent for discharges at two or more places as separate applications for consent for discharges at each of those places.

(2) Subject to the following section, it shall be the duty of a water authority to which an application for consent is made in pursuance of this section—

(a) to give the consent either unconditionally or subject to conditions or to refuse it; and

(b) not to withhold the consent unreasonably;

and if within the period of three months beginning with the date when an application for consent is received by a water authority, or within such longer period as may at any time be agreed upon in writing between the authority and the applicant, the authority has neither given nor refused the consent nor informed the applicant that the application has been transmitted to the Secretary of State in pursuance of the following section, the authority shall be deemed to have refused the consent.

(3) If it appears to a water authority that a person has, without the authority's consent, caused or permitted matter to be discharged in its area in contravention of section 32 (1) of this Act and that a similar contravention by that person is likely, the authority may if it thinks fit serve on him an instrument in writing giving its consent, subject to conditions specified in the instrument, for discharges of a kind so specified; but consent given in pursuance of this subsection shall not relate to any discharge which occurred before the instrument giving the consent was served on the recipient of the instrument.

(4) The conditions subject to which a water authority may give its consent in pursuance of this section shall be such reasonable conditions as the authority thinks fit; and without prejudice to the generality of the preceding provisions of this subsection those conditions may include reasonable conditions—

(a) as to the places at which the discharges to which the consent relates may be made and as to the design and construction of any outlets for the discharges;

(b) as to the nature, composition, temperature, volume and rate of the discharges and as to the periods during which the discharges may be made;

(c) as to the provision of facilities for taking samples of the matter discharged and in particular as to the provision, maintenance and use of manholes, inspection chambers, observation wells and boreholes in connection with the discharges;

(d) as to the provision, maintenance and testing of meters for measuring the volume and rate of the discharges and apparatus for determining the nature, composition and temperature of the discharges;

(e) as to the keeping of records of the nature, composition, temperature, volume and rate of the discharges and in particular of records of readings of meters and other recording apparatus provided in accordance with any other condition attached to the consent;

(f) as to the making of returns and the giving of other information to the water authority about the nature, composition, temperature, volume and rate of the discharges; and

(g) as to the steps to be taken for preventing the discharges from coming into contact with any specified underground water;

and it is hereby declared that consent may be given in pursuance of this section subject to different conditions in respect of different periods.

(5) A person who, in an application for consent in pursuance of this section, makes any statement which he knows to be false in a material particular or recklessly makes any statement which is false in a material particular shall be

guilty of an offence and liable on summary conviction to a fine not exceeding £400 or on conviction on indictment to imprisonment for a term not exceeding two years or a fine or both. [**63**]

DEFINITIONS

Water authority: Water Act 1973, s. 2

GENERAL NOTE

This section introduces a licensing system regulating the making of discharges of effluent into controlled waters, and replacing the similar, but somewhat more restricted, control of the Rivers (Prevention of Pollution) Act 1961. Consent given under this section will provide a defence to proceedings taken under s. 31 Consents under this section will not, however, prevent civil proceedings taken for an injunction or for damages by a riparian owner against the person responsible for the discharge ("pollution" of a stream such that proceedings may be taken in nuisance, is widely understood as common law: see *Young* v. *Bankier Distillery Co.*, [1893] A.C. 691).

It will be noted that the proposition that the making of a "new or altered outlet" for a discharge to a stream (as provided for in the Rivers (Prevention of Pollution) Acts 1951 and 1961, as amended by s. 17 of the Water Act 1973 and now repealed: Sch. 4) has been abandoned. Reliance for effective control is now placed on s. 31 and the present section, and also the requirement to obtain a consent and observe conditions imposed in a consent when so obtained.

A consent granted under this section may be made subject to reasonable conditions, and in particular subject to conditions of a kind listed in sub-s. (4). The Secretary of State may "call in" certain applications for consent for determination by himself (s. 35) and an appeal will lie to the Secretary of State, against a refusal of consent or against conditions imposed in a consent (s. 39). Before determining an application for consent, publicity must normally be given to the application (s. 36). A consent, once given, "runs with the land" and remains effective in relation to a particular discharge, by whomsoever exercised: sub-s. 36 (7). A consent under this section may afford a defence to proceedings taken under the statutes named in s. 54.

SUB-S. (1)

Presumably an application will be in writing, but no provision is included requiring a prescribed form to be used. Note that the application may relate to effluent of any kind; no reference is made in this section as to the waters into which the effluent is to be discharged, because there would be no point in applying for consent in relation to a discharge not affected by ss. 31 or 32. A consent once given may not normally be modified or varied under s. 37 within a period of two years without the agreement of the holder of the consent (see s. 38), but this restriction may not always apply (s. 38 (3)), and if a variation is so made compensation may be payable (see s. 38 (4)). Section 32 may also be exercised in circumstances envisaged in s. 41. As to notification of consents, see note to s. 38 (1).

SUB-S. (2)

As to conditions, see sub-s. (4). The period of three months will be extended if a person who has made written representations about an application has requested the Secretary of State to give directions calling in an application for his own determination: s. 36 (6).

SUB-S. (3)

Service of such an instrument should be effected in accordance with s. 95.

SUB-S. (4)

"Reasonable conditions": it would seem that, following the analogy of conditions attached to planning conditions, the courts would require any conditions imposed to relate to the prevention of water pollution, this being the *ratio legis* of these provisions: see, e.g. *Mixnam's Properties, Ltd.* v. *Chertsey Urban District Council*, [1965] A.C. 735; [1964] 2 All E.R. 627.

Taking of samples: any trade secrets obtained as a consequence of an exercise of this power on behalf of the water authority may not be divulged contrary to s. 94 (but see as to registers, s. 41).

35. Reference to Secretary of State of certain applications for consent

(1) The Secretary of State may, either in consequence of representations made to him or otherwise, direct a water authority to transmit to him for determination applications for consent in pursuance of the preceding section which are specified in the direction or are of a kind so specified, and it shall be the duty of the authority to comply with the direction and to inform each relevant applicant that his application has been transmitted to the Secretary of State.

(2) Before determining an application transmitted to him by a water authority in pursuance of this section the Secretary of State may if he thinks fit, and shall if a request to be heard with respect to the application is made to him in accordance with regulations by the applicant or the authority, cause a local inquiry to be held in pursuance of section 96 of this Act into the application or afford to the applicant and the authority an opportunity of appearing before and being heard by a person appointed by the Secretary of State for the purpose.

(3) Where in pursuance of the preceding subsection the Secretary of State affords to an applicant and a water authority an opportunity of appearing before and being heard by a person with respect to the application in question, it shall be the duty of the Secretary of State to afford an opportunity of appearing before and being heard by that person to any person who, in pursuance of subsection (1) (*c*) or (5) of the following section, has made representations relating to the application.

(4) It shall be the duty of the Secretary of State to determine an application transmitted to him by a water authority in pursuance of this section by directing the authority to refuse its consent in pursuance of the preceding section in consequence of the application or to give the consent either unconditionally or subject to such conditions as are specified in the direction, and it shall be the duty of the authority to comply with the direction. **[64]**

DEFINITION

Water authority: see Water Act 1973, s. 2.

GENERAL NOTE

Compare the called in procedure for planning applications under the Town and Country Planning Act 1971. "Directions" given under either sub-s. (1) or sub-s. (4), not being either orders or regulations, do not have to be made by way of statutory instruments. The Secretary of State may be requested under s. 36 (6) (*b*) to give directions under this section.

36. Provisions supplementary to ss. 34 and 35

(1) Where a water authority receives an application for consent in pursuance of section 34 of this Act or serves an instrument in pursuance of subsection (3) of

that section, it shall be the duty of the authority, before deciding whether to give or refuse consent in pursuance of the application or, as the case may be, after serving the instrument—

(*a*) to publish in the prescribed form notice of the application or instrument in two successive weeks in a newspaper or newspapers circulating in—

(i) the area or areas in which the places are situated at which it is proposed in the application that the discharges should be made or, as the case may be, at which discharges are the subject of consent given by the instrument, and

(ii) the area or areas appearing to the water authority to be in the vicinity of any stream or controlled waters which the authority considers likely to be affected by the discharges,

and, not earlier than the day following that on which the first publication of the notice is completed in all relevant areas in pursuance of the preceding provisions of this paragraph, to publish such a notice in the London Gazette;

(*b*) to send copies of the application or instrument to each local authority in whose area it is proposed in the application that a discharge should be made or in whose area a discharge is the subject of consent given by the instrument and, in the case of an application or instrument and, in the case of an application or instrument relating to controlled waters or an application relating to the sea outside controlled waters, to the Secretary of State and the Minister of Agriculture Fisheries and Food; and

(*c*) to consider any written representations relating to the application or instrument which are made to the authority by any person within the period of six weeks beginning with the date on which the notice of the application or instrument is published in the London Gazette;

and for the purposes of this subsection "local authority" means the council of a county or district, the Greater London Council, the council of a London borough and the Common Council of the City of London, and any place at sea at which it is proposed in an application that a discharge should be made shall be treated as situated at the point on land nearest to that place.

(2) [*Applies to Scotland only.*]

(3) Where notice of an application is published by a water authority in pursuance of subsection (1) (*a*) of this section, the authority shall be entitled to recover the cost of publication from the applicant.

(4) A water authority shall be entitled to disregard the provisions of subsection (1) of this section in relation to an application (except so much of paragraph (*b*) of that subsection as requires copies of the application to be sent to Ministers) if the authority proposes to give consent in pursuance of the application and considers that the discharges in question will have no appreciable effect on the water into which they are proposed to be made.

(5) The preceding provisions of this section shall have effect with prescribed modifications in relation to an application which is the subject of a direction in pursuance of subsection (1) of the preceding section.

(6) Where a water authority proposes to give consent in pursuance of section 34 of this Act in consequence of an application in respect of which representations have been made in pursuance of subsection (1) (*c*) of this section, then—

(*a*) it shall be the duty of the authority to serve notice of the proposal on the person who made the representations and to include in the notice a statement of the effect of the following paragraph; and

(*b*) that person may, within the period of twenty-one days beginning with the day on which the notice of the proposal is served on him, request the Secretary of State in accordance with regulations to give a direction in pursuance of subsection (1) of the preceding section in respect of the application; and

(*c*) it shall be the duty of the authority not to give consent in consequence of the application before the expiration of that period and, if within that period the said person makes a request in pursuance of the preceding paragraph and serves notice of the request on the authority, not to give consent in pursuance of the application unless the Secretary of State has given notice to the authority that he declines to comply with the request;

and in calculating in the case of any application the period of three months mentioned in section 34 (2) of this Act or a longer period there mentioned there shall be disregarded any period during which the water authority to which the application was made is prohibited by virtue of paragraph (*c*) of this subsection from giving consent in consequence of the application.

(7) A consent for any discharges which is given in pursuance of section 34 of this Act is not limited to discharges by a particular person and accordingly extends to the discharges in question which are made by any person.

(8) Regulations may provide that conditions of a prescribed kind to which a consent given in pursuance of section 34 of this Act is subject shall be disregarded for the purposes of sections 31 (2) (*a*), 32 (1) and 54 of this Act.

(9) A person who without reasonable excuse fails to comply with a condition which by virtue of the preceding subsection is to be disregarded for the purposes there mentioned shall be guilty of an offence and liable on summary conviction to a fine not exceeding £400; but no proceedings for such an offence shall be brought in England and Wales except by or with the consent of the Director of Public Prosecutions or by the water authority which gave the consent. **[65]**

DEFINITIONS

Controlled waters:	s. 56 (1)
Local authority:	see sub-s. (1)
Prescribed:	by regulations made by the Secretary of State: s. 105 (1)
Regulations:	of the Secretary of State: s. 105 (1)
Stream:	s. 56 (1) and s. 56 (3)
Water authority:	Water Act 1973, s. 2

GENERAL NOTE

This section, following the precedent for "noxious uses" in s. 26 of the Town and Country Planning Act 1971, provides for publicity to be given to applications for consent. There is, however, an important exception in sub-s. (4), and it is to be hoped that water authorities will not too readily consider that an application falls within this exception. Particular applications and consents (and the registers relating thereto) may be exempted from the requirements for publicity by means of a certificate obtained from the Secretary of State under s. 42.

SUB-S. (1)

If representations are made under this provision, the water authority must serve a notice under sub-s. (5) before giving consent to the application. The cost of publishing the application may be recovered from the applicant: sub-s. (3).

SUB-S. (5)

This refers to applications "called in" by the Secretary of State. Any determination made on a called in application is final, and not subject to further appeal: s. 39 (1).

SUB-S. (6)

Any notice under this subsection should be served in accordance with s. 95.

37. Revocation of consents and alteration and imposition of conditions

(1) It shall be the duty of a water authority by which a consent is given in pursuance of section 34 of this Act to review from time to time the consent and the conditions, if any, to which the consent is subject; and subject to the following section the authority may, by a notice served on the person making a discharge in pursuance of the consent, revoke the consent if it is reasonable to do so or make reasonable modifications of the said conditions or, in the case of an unconditional consent, provide that it shall be subject to reasonable conditions specified in the notice.

(2) Subject to the following section, the Secretary of State may, either in consequence of representations made to him or otherwise, direct a water authority to serve a notice in pursuance of the preceding subsection containing such provisions as are specified in the direction and it shall be the duty of the authority to comply with the direction; and if the authority fails to serve the notice within such period as the Secretary of State may allow he may, without prejudice to the generality of the powers conferred on him by section 97 of this Act or, in Scotland, section 211 of the Local Government (Scotland) Act 1973, serve the notice on behalf of the authority, and it is hereby declared that for the purposes of this Part of this Act a notice served on behalf of an authority by virtue of this subsection is served by the authority. **[66]**

DEFINITION

Water authority: Water Act 1973, s. 2

SUB-S. (1)

Service of a notice should be effected in accordance with s. 95.

"Reasonable" modifications: see comment on "reasonable conditions" in s. 34 (4).

Modification or revocation of a consent may not normally be made within a specified period of not less than two years without agreement (s. 33 (1)), but see s. 38 (3). It may also be the duty of the authority (under s. 46 (1)) to exercise their powers under the present subsection in certain circumstances. Note that compensation is *not* payable under s. 33 (4) as a consequence of this subsection.

SUB-S. (2)

"Representations": whether or not, apparently, they are made under s. 34 or within the six weeks period of s. 36 (1) (*c*).

"Direct": such a direction need not be made by statutory instrument.

Section 97 is the section giving general default powers to the Secretary of State. No compensation will be payable under s. 38 (4) if notice is served as a consequence of such a direction.

38. Restriction on variation and revocation of consent and of previous variation

(1) Each instrument signifying the consent of a water authority in pursuance of section 34 of this Act shall specify a period during which no notice in pursuance of subsection (1) of the preceding section is to be served in respect of the consent without the written agreement of a person making a discharge in pursuance of the consent; and the said period shall be a reasonable period of not less than two years beginning with the day on which the consent takes effect.

(2) Each notice served by a water authority in pursuance of subsection (1) of the preceding section (except a notice which only revokes a consent or conditions) shall specify a period during which a subsequent notice in pursuance of that subsection which alters the effect of the first-mentioned notice is not to be served without the written agreement of a person making a discharge in pursuance of the consent to which the first-mentioned notice relates; and the said period shall be a reasonable period of not less than two years beginning with the day on which the first-mentioned notice is served.

(3) Nothing in the preceding provisions of this section shall prohibit a notice in pursuance of subsection (1) of the preceding section from being served by a water authority, without such written agreement as is mentioned in those provisions and during the period specified in any relevant instrument or notice by virtue of those provisions, if the authority (or, in the case of a notice served by virtue of subsection (2) of that section, the Secretary of State) considers—

(*a*) that it is necessary to serve the notice in order to provide proper protection for persons likely to be affected by discharges which could lawfully be made apart from the notice; or

(*b*) in the case of a notice relating to a consent given by an instrument served in pursuance of subsection (3) of section 34 of this Act, that it is appropriate to serve the notice in consequence of representations received in pursuance of section 36 (1) of this Act with respect to the instrument.

(4) Where a notice is served by an authority by virtue of the preceding subsection, the authority shall be liable to pay compensation to the recipient of the notice unless it is served in pursuance of the said subsection (1) and not by virtue of the said subsection (2) and either—

(*a*) it states that in the opinion of the authority the notice is required—

(i) in consequence of a change of circumstances (which may include a change in the information available as to the discharges to which the notice relates or as to the interaction of those discharges with other discharges or matter) which has occurred since the day mentioned in subsection (1) or, as the case may be, subsection (2) of this section and could not reasonably have been foreseen on that day, and

(ii) otherwise than in consequence of consents given in pursuance of the said section 34 after that day,

and states the reasons for the opinion; or

(*b*) the relevant consent was given by an instrument served in pursuance of subsection (3) of the said section 34 and the notice is served during the period of three months beginning with the date on which notice of the instrument was published in the London Gazette in pursuance of section 36 (1) of this Act.

(5) Provision may be made by regulations as to the manner of determining the amount of any compensation payable in pursuance of this section including the factors to be taken into account in determining that amount. **[67]**

DEFINITIONS

Notices:	service should be effected in accordance with s. 95
Regulations:	made by the Secretary of State: s. 105 (1)
Water authority:	Water Act 1973, s. 2

SUB-S. (1)

This is the first place in the statute where any indication is given that a consent under s. 34 should be notified to the applicant. The consent is "given" when the authority takes the decision; the present subsection makes it clear that an "instrument" should then be prepared and (presumably) served in accordance with s. 95 on the applicant, informing him that the consent has been given, notifying him of the relevant conditions, and also containing the information required by the present subsection. The period(s) so specified or agreed may be ignored in circumstances specified in sub-s. (3).

SUB-S. (3)

This subsection permits a revocation or modification notice to be served before the end of the respective periods referred to in sub-ss. (1) and (2). If the notice is served otherwise than pursuant to sub-s. (1) or in accordance with a direction by the Secretary of State, compensation will be payable by the water authority under sub-s. (4).

"Proper protection": this clause has clearly been included in the statute to encourage riparian owners to make representations about an effluent in preference to taking proceedings for an injunction in respect of an alleged nuisance at common law.

The "said subsections (1) and (2)" are references to s. 37 (1) and 37 (2) respectively.

"Instrument under s. 34 (3)": this refers to the case where a discharge made without consent is legitimated by a consent given without application, but which then imposes enforceable conditions.

SUB-S. (4)

A person who has been served with a notice under s. 37 (1) containing a statement to the effect set out in this subsection, may request the Secretary of State to direct that the notice shall have effect as if the statement were omitted (s. 39 (3)). He will then be entitled to compensation under this subsection.

SUB-S. (5)

Presumably the regulations will also provide that any dispute is to be determined by arbitration under s. 31 (1) of the Arbitration Act 1950. Regulations may also be made to this effect under s. 45 (3).

39. Appeals to Secretary of State

(1) Any question as to whether—

(*a*) a water authority has unreasonably withheld its consent in pursuance of section 31 (3) or 34 of this Act or regulations made by virtue of section 31 (5) of this Act or has given its consent in pursuance of the said section 34 or such regulations subject to conditions which are unreasonable; or (*b*) a notice served in pursuance of section 37 (1) of this Act contains terms (other than a term required by subsection (2) of the preceding section) which are unreasonable; or

(*c*) the period specified in any instrument or notice in pursuance of subsection (1) or (2) of the preceding section is unreasonable,

shall, subject to the following subsection, be determined for the purposes of this Part of this Act by the Secretary of State; but no question relating to a determination of the Secretary of State in pursuance of section 35 (4) of this Act shall be referred to him in pursuance of this subsection and any such determination shall be final.

(2) Where the consent of a water authority in pursuance of regulations made by virtue of section 31 (5) of this Act is withheld for any activity or is given subject to conditions for any activity and the applicant for the consent obtains a certificate from the Minister of Agriculture, Fisheries and Food stating that the activity in question is a good agricultural practice, any question as to whether the water authority has unreasonably withheld the consent or given it subject to conditions which are unreasonable shall be determined for the purposes of this Part of this Act by the Secretary of State and the said Minister acting jointly.

This subsection shall not apply to Scotland.

(3) If a water authority serves on any person a notice in pursuance of section 37 of this Act which contains such a statement as is mentioned in paragraph (*a*) of subsection (4) of the preceding section, that person or another person authorised by him in that behalf may request the Secretary of State to direct that that subsection shall have effect in relation to the notice as if the statement were omitted and the Secretary of State may if he thinks fit comply with the request.

(4) Provision may be made by regulations as to the manner in which and the time within which a question may be referred or a request may be made in pursuance of the preceding provisions of this section and as to procedure for dealing with such a reference or request.

(5) In any case where—

(*a*) a question as to whether a water authority has unreasonably withheld its consent in pursuance of section 34 of this Act, or has given its consent in pursuance of that section subject to conditions which are unreasonable, is referred to the Secretary of State in pursuance of this section; and

(*b*) representations relating to the application for the consent in question were made to the authority in pursuance of section 36 (1) (*c*) of this Act,

it shall be the duty of the Secretary of State, before he determines the question, to secure that the authority has served notice of the reference on the persons who made the representations and to take account of any further written representations relating to the application which are received by him from those persons within a prescribed period.

(6) Where a question is referred to the Secretary of State in pursuance of subsection (1) of this section and he determines that the consent in question was unreasonably withheld or that the conditions or terms or period in question are or is unreasonable, he shall give to the relevant water authority such a direction as he thinks fit with regard to the consent, conditions, terms or period and it shall be the duty of the authority to comply with the direction; and the preceding provisions of this subsection shall apply to a reference in pursuance of

subsection (2) of this section as they apply to a reference in pursuance of subsection (1) of this section but as if for any reference in those provisions to the Secretary of State there were substituted a reference to him and the said Minister acting jointly.

(7) The withholding by a water authority of such a consent as is mentioned in subsection (1) of this section, the conditions subject to which such a consent is given and such terms and period as are so mentioned shall be treated as reasonable for the purposes of this Part of this Act until the contrary is determined in pursuance of subsection (1) or (2) of this section except that where a question as to the reasonableness of the conditions of a consent given in pursuance of regulations made by virtue of section 31 (5) of this Act is referred to the Secretary of State or to him and the said Minister in pursuance of this section the consent shall be treated for those purposes as unconditional while the reference is pending.

(8) At any stage of the proceedings on a reference to the Secretary of State or to him and the said Minister in pursuance of this section he or they may, and shall if so directed by the High Court or, in Scotland, the Court of Session, state in the form of a special case for the decision of the court any question of law arising in those proceedings; and in England and Wales the decision of the court on the special case shall be deemed to be a judgment of the court within the meaning of section 27 of the Supreme Court of Judicature (Consolidation) Act 1925 (which relates to the jurisdiction of the Court of Appeal to hear and determine appeals from any judgment of the High Court) but no appeal to the Court of Appeal shall be brought by virtue of this subsection except with the leave of that court or the High Court. [**68**]

DEFINITIONS

Notices:	service should be effected in accordance with s. 95
Mine:	s. 105 (1)
Quarry:	s. 105 (1)
Regulations:	made by the Secretary of State under s. 105 (1)
Water authority:	Water Act 1973, s. 2

GENERAL NOTE

This is the section providing for appeals to lie to the Secretary of State from decisions of the water authority under the licensing system contained in Part II. The Secretary of State may decide to hold a local inquiry under s. 96 on any reference or request under this section, but he cannot be compelled to do so, although the procedure to be followed may be provided for by the regulations to be made under sub-s. (4). Sub-s. (8) is the only provision in this Act making express provision for an appeal to lie to the High Court (by case stated on a point of law) from a determination of the Secretary of State.

SUB-S. (1)

Section 31 (3) refers to the deposit of solid refuse of a mine or quarry; s. 34 is the substantive provision regarding the grant of consents for the discharge of effluent; regulations under s. 31 (5) refer to the prohibition without consent of prescribed activities in a particular area (see s. 31 (1)); s. 37 (1) refers to the revocation or modification of consent.

SUB-S. (2)

"Good agricultural practice": but see s. 51. See also sub-s. (6) of this section.

SUB-S. (7)

This apparently amounts to a clause excluding the jurisdiction of the courts to adjudicate on the question of "reasonableness' before there has been a reference or request to the Secretary of State. Therefore it would seem that *certiorari* would not lie to a water authority on this ground (contrast *R.* v. *Hillingdon London Borough Council, ex parte Royco Homes Ltd.*, [1974] 2 All E.R. 643, a planning case).

SUB-S. (8)

"Question of law": this includes the question whether or not the Secretary of State has jurisdiction in a specific case; see *May and Hassall Ltd.* v. *Vsesojuznoje Objedinenije Exportles* (*No.* 2) (1941), 46 Com. Cas. 221.

"Leave": may be given as to one point only, or subject to conditions as to costs: see *Jones* v. *Bernstein*, [1900] 1 Q.B. 100; *Great Western Rail. Co.* v. *Wills*, [1917] A.C. 148.

The procedural provisions implementing this subsection are contained in R.S.C. Ord. 56, rr. 7–12, and as to the obtaining of leave, see R.S.C. Ord. 59, r. 14.

[The subsection is copied from s. 6 (5) of the Rivers (Prevention of Pollution) Act 1961.]

40. Transitional provisions relating to consents

(1) Regulations may provide—

(*a*) for any consent for discharges which was given in pursuance of the Rivers (Prevention of Pollution) Acts 1951 to 1961 or the Rivers (Prevention of Pollution) (Scotland) Acts 1951 and 1965 or section 72 of the Water Resources Act 1963 to have effect for any of the purposes of this Part of this Act as if given in pursuance of prescribed provisions of section 34 of this Act; and

(*b*) for any conditions to which such a consent was subject in pursuance of any of those enactments to have effect for any of those purposes as if attached to the consent in pursuance of prescribed provisions of this Part of this Act.

(2) Regulations may provide for the terms of a consent for an outlet which was given in pursuance of the Rivers (Prevention of Pollution) Act 1951 and for conditions to which such a consent was subject in pursuance of that Act or which were imposed with respect to the outlet in pursuance of section 7 (4) of that Act—

(*a*) to have effect, with or without modifications, for any of the purposes of this Part of this Act as if the terms or conditions were conditions attached to a consent given in pursuance of section 34 of this Act for discharges from the outlet; or

(*b*) to be treated, with or without modifications, for any of those purposes in such other manner as may be prescribed.

. . . . .

(3) An application for such a consent as is mentioned in subsection (1) of this section which is pending immediately before the relevant day shall be treated on and after that day as an application for consent in pursuance of section 34 of this Act which was made on the day on which it was actually made.

(4) Where an application for consent in pursuance of section 34 of this

Act in respect of any discharge is duly made to a water authority before the relevant day and the discharge in question is not such as is mentioned in section 32 (3) (*a*) of this Act and is substantially a continuation of a previous discharge which during the year ending with the 30th April 1974 was lawfully made without such consent as is so mentioned (any reduction of the temperature, volume or rate of the discharge as compared with that of the previous discharge being disregarded), the authority shall be deemed to have given unconditionally the consent applied for—

(*a*) until the authority actually gives the consent unconditionally; or

(*b*) if the authority decides to refuse consent or to give it subject to conditions, until the expiration of the period of three months beginning with the date when the authority serves on the applicant notice of the decision; or

(*c*) if during that period the applicant appeals to the Secretary of State against the decision in pursuance of the preceding section, until the determination of the appeal.

(5) Regulations may provide for any appeal which immediately before the relevant day is pending in pursuance of the Rivers (Prevention of Pollution) Acts 1951 to 1961, the Rivers (Prevention of Pollution) (Scotland) Acts 1951 and 1965 or section 72 (3) of the said Act of 1963 to be treated on and after that day as an appeal in pursuance of prescribed provisions of this Part of this Act.

(6) In this section "the relevant day" means the day when section 32 (1) of this Act comes into force. **[69]**

DEFINITIONS

Regulations:	made by the Secretary of State under s. 105 (1)
Relevant day:	see sub-s. (6)
Water authority:	Water Act 1973, s. 2, as successor to the river authority established by the Water Resources Act 1963

GENERAL NOTE

The words omitted from sub-s. (2) at the place indicated by dots apply to Scotland only.

This section enables regulations to be made providing for consents under the former legislation to continue in force as if they were consents under this Act. Subsection (3) deals with pending applications. See also s. 56 (5).

Ancillary provisions relating to control of discharges

41. Registers

(1) It shall be the duty of water authorities to maintain, in accordance with regulations, registers containing prescribed particulars of—

(*a*) applications for consents made to the authorities in pursuance of this Part of this Act;

(*b*) consents given in pursuance of any provision of this Part of this Act (except section 40 (4)) and the conditions to which the consents are subject;

(*c*) samples of effluent taken by the authorities in pursuance of section 113 (1) of the Water Resources Act 1963 or, in Scotland, section 19 of the Rivers (Prevention of Pollution) (Scotland) Act 1951, samples of water taken by the authorities, information produced by analyses of the samples and the steps taken in consequence of the information;

(*d*) certificates issued in pursuance of the following section;

(*e*) notices of which copies have been served on the authorities in pursuance of section 51 (3) (*b*) of this Act other than notices of rejections of applications.

(2) It shall be the duty of a water authority—

(*a*) to secure that registers maintained by the authority in pursuance of the preceding subsection are, after such date as is prescribed with respect to the registers, open to inspection by the public free of charge at all reasonable hours; and

(*b*) to afford members of the public reasonable facilities for obtaining from the authority, on payment of reasonable charges, copies of entries in the register. **[70]**

DEFINITIONS

Regulations:	made by the Secretary of State under s. 105 (1)
Water authority:	Water Act 1973, s. 2

GENERAL NOTE

Compare this requirement for the maintenance of registers with those maintained under s. 7 of the Rivers (Prevention of Pollution) Act, 1951 (as amended by s. 7 of the Act of the same name of 1961) which the present Act repeals (Sch. 4). If information as to samples, etc., is given in accordance with the regulations, there can be no question of an offence against s. 94 (but see s. 42).

42. Power of Secretary of State to exempt applications, consents and conditions, etc., from publicity.

(1) If a person who proposes to make or has made an application to a water authority for any consent in pursuance of section 34 of this Act (hereafter in this subsection referred to as "the relevant application')—

(*a*) applies to the Secretary of State within a prescribed period for a certificate providing that section 36 (1) of this Act and paragraphs (*a*) to (*c*) and (*e*) of subsection (1) of the preceding section shall not apply to the relevant application or to any consent given or conditions imposed in consequence of the relevant application or to any sample of effluent taken from a discharge for which consent is given in consequence of the relevant application or to information produced by analysis of such a sample; and

(*b*) satisfies the Secretary of State that it would—

(i) prejudice to an unreasonable degree some private interest by disclosing information about a trade secret, or

(ii) be contrary to the public interest,

if a certificate were not issued in pursuance of his application to the Secretary of State,

the Secretary of State may issue a certificate to that person providing that section 36 (1) of this Act and those paragraphs shall not apply to such of the things mentioned in paragraph (*a*) of this subsection as are specified in the certificate.

(2) If a person who is making or proposes to make a discharge which is the subject of a consent given in pursuance of the Rivers (Prevention of Pollution) Acts 1951 to 1961 or the Rivers (Prevention of Pollution) (Scotland) Acts 1951 and 1965 or section 72 of the Water Resources Act 1963—

(*a*) applies to the Secretary of State for a certificate providing that subsection (1) (*b*) or (*c*) of the preceding section shall not apply to the consent or any conditions to which the consent is subject or any sample of effluent taken from a discharge to which the consent relates or any information produced by analysis of such a sample; and

(*b*) satisfies the Secretary of State as mentioned in paragraph (*b*) of the preceding subsection,

the Secretary of State may issue a certificate to that person providing that the said subsection (1) (*b*) or (*c*) shall not apply to such of the things mentioned in paragraph (*a*) of this subsection as are specified in the certificate. [**71**]

DEFINITIONS

Prescribed:	by regulations: s. 105 (1)
Regulations:	made by the Secretary of State: s. 105 (1)
Water authority:	Water Act 1973, s. 2

Control of discharges of trade effluent into public sewers

43. Control of discharges into sewers

(1) No discharge of trade effluent from any trade premises into a sewer of a water authority shall after the appointed day be authorised by virtue of—

(*a*) section 4 of the Public Health (Drainage of Trade Premises) Act 1937 (which relates to certain cases in which discharges were lawfully made before the passing of that Act or before the alteration of the relevant sewerage system); or

(*b*) any agreement which is mentioned in section 7 (4) of that Act (under which any agreement with respect to any trade effluent which was duly made between a local authority and the owner or occupier of any trade premises before the commencement of that Act is not affected by that Act) and which does not contain express provision enabling the authority to terminate the agreement, so far as it relates to discharges of trade effluent into the sewer of the authority, whether or not there is a breach of the agreement by a person other than the authority;

and accordingly subsections (1) to (3) of the said section 4 shall cease to have effect at the end of the appointed day.

(2) Where any discharges of trade effluent from any premises in the area of a water authority into a sewer were authorised by virtue of the said section 4 or such an agreement immediately before the date of the passing of this Act and the owner or occupier of the premises gives notice to the authority within the period of six months beginning with that date stating that such discharges from the premises were so authorised, consent shall be deemed to be duly given on the appointed day by the authority for such discharges from the premises into the sewer after that day as were authorised by virtue of the said section 4 or the agreement immediately before the date aforesaid and shall be deemed to be so given subject to the same conditions (if any) as to charges or otherwise as—

(*a*) in the case of discharges authorised by virtue of the said section 4, the conditions to which by virtue of an agreement (whether subsisting or not) or of a direction given in pursuance of section 55 or 57 of the Public Health Act 1961 (which relate to charges and to conditions dealing with other matters) the discharges were subject immediately before the appointed day; and (*b*) in the case of discharges authorised by an agreement mentioned in the said section 7 (4), the conditions to which the discharges were subject immediately before the appointed day.

(3) The water authority whose consent for any discharge is deemed to be given by virtue of the preceding subsection may at any time after the appointed day, and shall if the authority is requested after the appointed day to do so by any person entitled to make a discharge in pursuance of the consent, by a notice served on the owner and any occupier of the premises in question cancel the deemed consent and, subject to the following subsection, give its actual consent for such discharges as were authorised by the deemed consent.

(4) An actual consent given in pursuance of the preceding subsection shall be so given either unconditionally or subject to any conditions which under section 2 (3) of the said Act of 1937 (including section 59 of the said Act of 1961) may be attached to consents, any reference to a trade effluent notice in paragraphs (*a*) and (*d*) of the said section 2 (3) being construed for the purposes of this subsection as a reference to the actual consent; and the notice signifying the actual consent shall indicate that a right of appeal is conferred by virtue of the following subsection in respect of the notice.

(5) A person on whom notice is served in pursuance of subsection (3) of this section may, in accordance with regulations, appeal to the Secretary of State against the notice; and on any such appeal the Secretary of State may give to the water authority in question such a direction as he thinks fit with respect to the notice and it shall be the duty of the authority to comply with the direction.

(6) Provision may be made by regulations with respect to consents and the conditions of consents for discharges of trade effluent into a sewer of a water authority through a drain or sewer provided after the appointed day by the authority in pursuance of section 42 of the Public Health Act 1936 (which enables a water authority to close certain drains and sewers if it provides alternative drains or sewers which are equally convenient).

(7) This section does not apply to Scotland. **[72]**

DEFINITIONS

Appointed day:	s. 44 (5)
Drain:	Public Health Act 1936, s. 343 (1)
Owner:	s. 105 (1)
Premises:	s. 105 (1)
Regulations:	made by the Secretary of State: s. 105 (1)
Sewer:	Public Health Act 1936, s. 343 (1)
Trade effluent:	s. 105 (1)
Trade premises:	Public Health (Drainage of Trade Premises) Act 1937, s. 14
Water authority:	Water Act 1973, s. 2

GENERAL NOTE

This section was bought into force on 12th December 1974 by The Control of Pollution Act 1974 (Commencement No. 1) Order 1974 (S.I. 1974 No. 2039). With s. 44 and s. 45, it brings fully into the normal control of the Public Health (Drainage of Trade Premises) Act 1937, "prescriptive discharges" of such effluent, i.e. those that were being made before the coming into force of the 1937 Act. These sections allow existing conditions to continue temporarily by the device of a "deemed consent", and then allow the water authority to serve notice of an "actual consent" at any time after a specified day (see sub-s. (3) and s. 44 (5)); this will have the effect of imposing new conditions and charges in respect of the discharge. These sections replace the limited controls over prescriptive discharges contained in ss. 55–58 of the Public Health Act 1961 (repealed by Sch. 4); the power to impose specified conditions in a trade effluent consent contained in s. 59 of the 1961 Act is not affected by the present Act, although the administration of the trade effluent legislation is now the responsibility of the water authorities by virtue of the Water Act 1973.

Regulations may be made as to charges to be imposed for facilities provided in respect of discharges pursuant to consents under this section or under the 1937 Act: s. 52.

SUB-S. (2)

Service of a notice should be effected in accordance with s. 95. Any such deemed consent comes into effect automatically without any action on behalf of the water authority but see sub-s. (3). See also s. 44 (1).

SUB-S. (3)

Service of a notice should be effected in accordance with s. 95. Notification must be given of the right of appeal under sub-s. (5): see sub-s. (4).

SUB-S. (4)

But see s. 44 (2).

44. Provisions supplementary to s. 43

(1) It is hereby declared that a direction may be given in pursuance of subsection (1) of section 60 of the Public Health Act 1961 varying the conditions attached to an actual consent given in pursuance of the preceding section and that the other provisions of Part V of that Act have effect accordingly.

(2) Notwithstanding anything in subsection (4) of the preceding section or the preceding subsection, where a deemed consent is cancelled by a notice giving an actual consent in pursuance of subsection (3) of the preceding section and the deemed consent was by virtue of subsection (2) of the preceding section subject to a condition which was the same as one imposed by a direction given in pursuance of section 55 or 57 of the said Act of 1961, then—

(*a*) in a case where the condition related to charges, a different condition as to charges, and

(*b*) in a case where the condition did not relate to charges, a different condition as to any matter except charges,

shall not, except with the written agreement of the owner and any occupier of the premises in question or in pursuance of the following section, be attached to the actual consent during the period during which, by virtue of subsection (3) of the said section 55 or subsection (2) of the said section 57, no further direction to the said owner or occupier in pursuance of that section in respect of charges or, as the case may be, in respect of other matters could have been given without his consent if the said section 55 or 57 had remained in force.

(3) Provision may be made by regulations—

(*a*) for determining by arbitration or otherwise whether any such agreement as is mentioned in subsection (1) (*b*) of the preceding section relates also to a matter other than the discharge of trade effluent into a sewer of a particular water authority;

(*b*) for determining as aforesaid what modifications (if any) of such an agreement relating also to such a matter are appropriate in consequence of any prescribed provision of the preceding section;

(*c*) where the conditions mentioned in paragraph (*b*) of subsection (2) of the preceding section include a condition as to charges which are in respect of the discharges in question and other matters, for determining as aforesaid the proportion of the charges attributable to the discharges and for limiting accordingly the conditions to which the discharges are, for the purposes of that paragraph, to be treated as subject immediately before the appointed day.

(4) Section 70 of the said Act of 1961 (which provides for a copy of each direction given by a water authority in pursuance of Part V of that Act to be kept available for inspection and copying by any person at all reasonable times) shall apply to a notice given in pursuance of subsection (3) of the preceding section as it applies to such a direction.

(5) In the preceding section and this section "the appointed day" means such day after the expiration of six months beginning with the date on which this Act is passed as the Secretary of State may by order appoint; and an expression used in any provision of the preceding section or this section and in the said Act of 1937 has the same meaning in that provision as in that Act.

(6) This section does not apply to Scotland. [**73**]

DEFINITIONS

Appointed day:	see sub-s. (5)
Owner:	s. 105 (1)
Premises:	s. 105 (1)
Regulations:	made by the Secretary of State under s. 105 (1)

GENERAL NOTE

This section was brought into force on 12th December 1974 by The Control of Pollution Act 1974 (Commencement No. 1) Order 1974 (S.I. 1974 No. 2039).

SUB-S. (2)

The period referred in s. 55 and s. 57 (2) of the Public Health Act 1961 is two years, unless the period has been extended by agreement.

SUB-S. (3)

Any arbitration should be conducted in accordance with the Arbitration Act 1950; see s. 31 (1) thereof.

SUB-S. (5)

Any such order will not be subject to the negative resolution procedure in Parliament: see s. 104 (1).

45. Early variation of conditions of discharges

(1) Notwithstanding anything in subsection (2) of section 60 of the Public Health Act 1961 (under which a water authority may not, except with the direction under subsection (1) of that section varying the conditions of its consent to the discharge of trade effluent into a public sewer within two years from the date of the consent or of notice of a previous direction), a water authority may give such a direction within the period mentioned in the said subsection (2) without such written consent as aforesaid if the authority considers it necessary to do so in order to provide proper protection for persons likely to be affected by discharges which could lawfully be made apart from the direction.

(2) Where a water authority gives such a direction by virtue of the preceding subsection, the authority shall be liable to pay compensation to the owner and occupier of the trade premises to which the direction relates unless the authority is of opinion that the direction is required—

(*a*) in consequence of a change of circumstances (which may include a change in the information available as to the discharges to which the consent in question relates or as to the interaction of those discharges with other discharges or matter) which has occurred since the beginning of the period of two years in question and could not reasonably have been foreseen at the beginning of that period; and

(*b*) otherwise than in consequence of consents for discharges given after the beginning of that period;

and where the authority is of such an opinion it shall be the duty of the authority to give to the owner and occupier of the said premises notice of its reasons for the opinion.

(3) Subsection (5) of section 38 of this Act shall have effect as if the reference to that section included a reference to this section.

(4) A person to whom notice is given in pursuance of subsection (2) of this section may, in accordance with regulations, appeal to the Secretary of State against the notice on the ground that compensation should be paid in consequence of the direction to which the notice relates; and on any such appeal the Secretary of State may direct that that subsection shall have effect as if the authority had not been of the opinion to which the notice relates.

(5) This section does not apply to Scotland. [**74**]

DEFINITIONS

Owner:	s. 105 (1)
Public sewer:	Public Health Act 1936, s. 20 (1) as amended by the Water Act 1973, and s. 343 (1) of the 1936 Act.
Regulations:	made by the Secretary of State: s. 105 (1)
Trade effluent:	s. 105 (1)
Trade premises:	Public Health (Drainage of Trade Premises) Act 1937, s. 14 (1)
Water authority:	Water Act 1973, s. 2

SUB-S. (1)

The period under s. 60 (2) of the 1961 Act is normally two years from the date of the consent.

"Proper protection": compare the procedure of s. 38 (3).

SUB-S. (2)

Any such notice should be served in accordance with s. 95. There is a right of appeal to the Secretary of State: see sub-s. (4).

Miscellaneous

46. Operations by water authorities to remedy or forestall pollution of water

(1) Where it appears to a water authority that pollution injurious to the fauna or flora of a stream in its area has been caused in consequence of discharges made by virtue of a consent given by the authority in pursuance of section 34 of this Act after the date when this section comes into force or discharges made by virtue of a variation of a consent in pursuance of that section which was made by the authority after that date, then, subject to the following subsection, it shall be the duty of the authority—

(a) to exercise the powers conferred on it by section 37 (1) of this Act with a view to ensuring that further discharges of a kind which caused the injurious pollution in question are not made by virtue of the consent or variation or are not so made after such a period as the authority considers necessary for the purpose of allowing a person making discharges by virtue of the consent or variation to secure that the discharges are not of such a kind or to make arrangements for discontinuing the discharges; and

(b) in a case where the authority considers that a period is necessary for the purpose aforesaid, to carry out as soon as reasonably practicable such operations as the authority considers appropriate with a view to remedying or mitigating the injurious pollution in question; and

(c) to carry out, as soon as reasonably practicable or after the expiration of the said period, such operations as are necessary for the purpose of restoring the fauna and flora of the stream, so far as it is reasonably practicable to do so, to the state in which they were immediately before discharges were made by virtue of the consent or variation.

(2) If it appears to a water authority that injurious pollution of a stream in its area has been caused in consequence of discharges made as mentioned in the preceding subsection but that further discharges so made after such a period as the authority considers reasonable in the circumstances will, after the carrying out of such operations as are mentioned in paragraph (c) of that subsection, not cause injurious pollution of the stream, then—

(a) the authority shall not be required by virtue of paragraph (a) of the preceding subsection to exercise the powers there mentioned; but

(b) it shall be the duty of the authority—

(i) to carry out as soon as reasonably practicable such operations as are mentioned in paragraph (b) of the preceding subsection, and

(ii) to carry out, after the expiration of the period mentioned in the preceding provisions of this subsection, such operations as are mentioned in paragraph (c) of the preceding subsection.

(3) The duty imposed on a water authority by virtue of subsection (1) (a) of this section shall be performed notwithstanding anything in subsections (1) and (2) of section 38 of this Act; but—

(a) where in the performance of that duty a notice is served in consequence of which compensation would have been payable in pursuance of subsection (4) of that section if the notice had been served by virtue of subsection (3) of that section, compensation shall be so payable as if the notice had been so served; and

(b) nothing in this section shall be construed as restricting the powers conferred on the Secretary of State by section 37 (2) of this Act.

(4) Where it appears to a water authority that any poisonous, noxious or polluting matter or any solid waste matter is likely to enter, or is or was present in, any relevant waters in its area, the authority may, without prejudice to any duty imposed on it by virtue of the preceding provisions of this section, carry out in its area or elsewhere such operations as it considers appropriate—

(a) in a case where the matter appears likely to enter such waters, for the purpose of preventing it from doing so; and

(b) in a case where the matter appears to be or to have been present in such waters, for the purpose of removing or disposing of the matter or of remedying or mitigating any pollution caused by its presence in the waters or of restoring the waters (including the fauna and flora in them), so far as it is reasonably practicable to do so, to the state in which they were immediately before the matter became present in the waters;

but nothing in this subsection empowers a water authority to impede or prevent the making of any discharge in pursuance of a consent given by any authority by virtue of section 34 of this Act.

(5) Where a water authority carries out any operations in pursuance of this section the authority shall, subject to the following subsection, be entitled to recover the costs of doing so—

(*a*) in the case of operations in pursuance of subsection (1) or (2) of this section, from the persons who made the discharges in question; and

(*b*) in the case of operations in pursuance of the preceding subsection, from any persons who caused or knowingly permitted the matter in question to be present at the place from which it was likely in the opinion of the authority to enter the relevant waters or, as the case may be, to be present in the relevant waters.

(6) No such costs shall be payable by a person—

(*a*) in so far as he satisfies the court in which it is sought to recover the costs that the costs were incurred unnecessarily; or

(*b*) for any operations in respect of water from an abandoned mine which that person permitted to reach such a place as is mentioned in paragraph (*b*) of the preceding subsection or to enter relevant waters; or

(*c*) if he is a person to whom compensation is payable by virtue of subsection (3) of this section in respect of a consent to which the operations in question relate.

(7) In determining the damage which a person has suffered in consequence of pollution in respect of which operations have been or may be carried out in pursuance of this section, account shall be taken of the extent to which it is shown that the damage has been reduced by operations in pursuance of this section and of the extent to which it is shown that the damage is likely to be so reduced.

(8) In this section—

"injurious pollution", in relation to a stream, means pollution injurious to the fauna or flora of the stream; and

"variation", in relation to a consent, means a modification in pursuance of subsection (1) of section 37 of this Act of the conditions to which the consent is subject or, in the case of an unconditional consent, the subjection of the consent to conditions in pursuance of that subjection. **[75]**

DEFINITIONS

Area:	s. 56 (4)
Caused or knowingly permitted:	see comment on s. 31 (1)
Injurious pollution:	sub-s. (8)
Reasonably practicable:	see comment on s. 31 (3)
Relevant waters:	s. 31 (1)
Stream:	s. 56 (1) and s. 56 (3)
Water authority:	Water Act 1973, s. 2

GENERAL NOTE

This section enables a water authority to take precautionary or salvage action where injurious pollution of a stream is feared or has actually occurred. First they may have a duty to modify or revoke an existing s. 34 consent (but they may not do this unnecessarily: see sub-s. (2)). Then they may carry out operations so as to remedy or mitigate the pollution, and they may, if reasonably practicable, restore the fauna and flora of the stream. They can also take action to prevent polluting matter entering relevant waters (sub-s. (4)), and in certain circumstances recover their costs thereby incurred (sub-s. (5) and (6)).

The duties imposed under this section may be enforceable by the default powers of the Secretary of State under s. 97.

SUB-S. (1)

Note that this subsection is confined in its operation to *streams*, and does not apply to all "relevant waters". If the pollution is caused otherwise than by a consensual discharge, the authority will have to use not this power, but those given by sub-s. (4). Costs incurred under this subsection may be recoverable but not in cases where compensation is payable under sub-s. (3); see sub-ss. (5) and (6). This subsection should be read together with sub-s. (2).

No compensation will be payable under s. 33 in respect of action taken under sub-s. (1) (*a*): sub-s. (3).

SUB-S. (4)

As to floating debris in a stream, see s. 49.

SUB-S. (5)

But see sub-s. (6). Establishment charges may be added to any costs so recoverable: s. 90.

SUB-S. (7)

This refers to common law actions for damages, and see s. 105 (2).

47. Duty of water authorities to deal with waste from vessels, etc.

(1) It shall be the duty of each water authority—

(*a*) to arrange for the collection and disposal of waste from vessels in its area which appears to the authority to need collection in consequence of the provisions of section 33 of this Act; and

(*b*) to arrange for the provision of facilities for the washing out of prescribed appliances from vessels in its area.

(2) A water authority may arrange for the provision of facilities by way of water closets, urinals and wash basins for the use of persons from vessels in the authority's area.

(3) A port health authority shall have power to make arrangements with a water authority for the purposes of any of the preceding provisions of this section.

[76]

DEFINITIONS

Area:	s. 56 (4)
Prescribed:	by regulations made by the Secretary of State: s. 105 (1)
Vessels:	s. 105 (1)
Waste:	*not* defined for the purposes of Part II
Water authority:	Water Act 1973, s. 2

GENERAL NOTE

Subsection (1) imposes a duty, enforceable if necessary by the default action of the Secretary of State under s. 97; sub-s. (2) confers a power. A port health authority may have a similar power: see sub-s. (3).

48. Power of water authorities to exclude unregistered vessels from rivers, etc.

(1) Where it appears to a water authority to be appropriate to do so for the purpose of preventing the pollution of streams in its area, the authority may make byelaws providing that vessels shall not be on any such streams which are specified in the byelaws unless the vessels are registered by the authority in accordance with the byelaws or are exempted by the byelaws from registration; and a person who causes or knowingly permits a vessel to be on a stream in contravention of byelaws made by virtue of this subsection shall be guilty of an offence and liable on summary conviction to a fine not exceeding £50.

(2) Byelaws made by a water authority in pursuance of the preceding subsection may authorise the authority to make reasonable charges in respect of the registration of vessels in pursuance of the byelaws; and no charges shall be payable, by persons in or from vessels registered by the authority in pursuance of the byelaws, in respect of the use by those persons of facilities provided in pursuance of the preceding section by or by arrangement with the authority.
[77]

DEFINITIONS

Area:	s. 56 (4)
Stream:	s. 56 (1) and s. 56 (3)
Vessel:	s. 105 (1)
Water authority:	Water Act 1973, s. 2

GENERAL NOTE

Byelaws providing for registration of vessels under this section must be designed with the object of preventing pollution, and not (for example) for the improvement of navigation. The byelaws could presumably be more stringent than the provisions of s. 33. The byelaws must be made in accordance with the provisions of s. 36 (3) and Sch. 7, Part II of the Water Act 1973, and will therefore be subject to confirmation by the Secretary of State.

49. Deposits and vegetation in rivers, etc.

(1) If without the consent of the relevant water authority, which shall not be unreasonably withheld,—

(*a*) a person removes from any part of the channel or bed of a stream a deposit accumulated by reason of any dam, weir or sluice holding back the water of the stream and does so by causing the deposit to be carried away in suspension in the water of the stream; or

(*b*) any substantial amount of vegetation cut or uprooted in a stream, or so near to the stream that it falls into it, is allowed to remain in the stream by the wilful default of any person,

then, subject to the following subsection, that person shall be guilty of an offence and liable on summary conviction to a fine not exceeding £200.

(2) Nothing in paragraph (*a*) of the preceding subsection applies to anything done in the exercise of statutory powers conferred by or under any enactment relating to land drainage, flood prevention or navigation.

(3) Regulations may provide that any reference to a stream in subsection (1) of this section shall be construed as including a reference to such controlled waters as are prescribed for the purposes of that subsection.

(4) Any question as to whether the consent of a water authority in pursu-

ance of subsection (1) of this section is unreasonably withheld shall be determined by the Secretary of State; and any consent given in pursuance of section 4 of the Rivers (Prevention of Pollution) Act 1951 or section 24 of the Rivers (Prevention of Pollution) (Scotland) Act 1951 (which are superseded by this section) shall be treated for the purposes of this section as given in pursuance of this section. [**78**]

DEFINITIONS

Controlled waters:	s. 56 (1)
Prescribed:	by regulations: s. 105 (1)
Regulations:	made by the Secretary of State: s. 105 (1)
Stream:	s. 56 (1) and s. 56 (3)
Water authority:	Water Act 1973, s. 2

SUB-S. (1)

"unreasonably withheld": see sub-s. (4). Section 4 of the 1951 Act is repealed by Sch. 4.

50. Investigation of water pollution problems arising from closure of mines

Each water authority shall have power to carry out studies for the purpose of ascertaining—

(*a*) what problems relating to the pollution of relevant waters may arise or have arisen in consequence of the abandonment of any mine in its area or might arise if any such mine were abandoned; and

(*b*) what steps are likely to be appropriate for the purpose of dealing with the problems and what the cost of taking those steps would be. [**79**]

DEFINITIONS

Area:	s. 56 (4)
Mine:	s. 105 (1)
Relevant waters:	s. 31 (1)
Water authority:	Water Act 1973, s. 2

GENERAL NOTE

This section supplements the general power to obtain information given to all "relevant authorities" (including water authorities) by s. 93.

51. Notice to abstain from certain agricultural practices

(1) If a water authority is of opinion that any relevant waters—

(*a*) have been or are likely to be polluted in consequence of such an act or omission as is first mentioned in section 31 (2) (*c*) of this Act which has occurred at a place in the area of the authority; or

(*b*) are likely to be polluted if such an act or omission occurs at such a place,

the authority may, by an application in writing made to the Secretary of State which specifies the kind of act or omission in question and the reasons for the opinion, request the Secretary of State to serve on the occupier of the place a notice requesting the occupier to prevent acts or omissions of that kind at the place.

(2) It shall be the duty of an authority which makes an application in

pursuance of the preceding subsection to serve a copy of the application on the Minister of Agriculture, Fisheries and Food and the occupier of the place to which the application relates and to serve on the said occupier a statement informing him that he may, within the period of twenty-eight days beginning with the date on which the statement is served on him, make representations in writing to the Secretary of State about the application.

. . . . .

(3) Where an application is made to the Secretary of State in pursuance of this section it shall be his duty, after considering any representations about the application which are made to him in pursuance of the preceding subsection—

(*a*) to serve on the occupier of the place in question the notice requested by the application or a notice containing a request to the occupier which the Secretary of State considers is less restrictive than the request specified in the application or a notice stating that he has rejected the application; and

(*b*) to serve on the authority in question a copy of the notice which the Secretary of State has served in pursuance of the preceding paragraph.

(4) It shall be the duty of a water authority which is required by virtue of section 41 (1) (*e*) of this Act to maintain a register containing particulars of notices of which copies have been served on the authority in pursuance of the preceding subsection to enter in the register, forthwith after the service on the authority of each such copy other than a copy of a notice of rejection of an application, particulars of the notice and a statement of the date on which it was served on the authority.

(5) If the Secretary of State considers that a notice served in pursuance of subsection (3) of this section on the occupier of a place should be cancelled he may, after giving notice of his proposal to do so to the water authority on whose application the other notice was served and considering any representations made to him by the authority about the proposal, serve on the occupier of the place a further notice cancelling the other notice at a time specified in the further notice; and where the Secretary of State serves a notice in pursuance of this subsection—

(*a*) it shall be his duty to serve a copy of it on the authority aforesaid; and

(*b*) it shall be the duty of the authority to enter in the said register a statement that the other notice was or is to be cancelled at the time specified as aforesaid. **[80]**

DEFINITIONS

Area:	s. 56 (4)
Relevant waters:	s. 31 (1)
Water authority:	Water Act 1973, s. 2

GENERAL NOTE

This section enables the Secretary of State on the application of the water authority to serve a notice on the occupier of a "place", requesting him to abstain from certain acts or omissions which may otherwise be "good agriculture practice" and so afford a defence to proceedings under s. 31 (1). Notices under this section should be served on the water authority in accordance with s. 95; that section does not apply to notices served by the Secretary of State on other persons, but it does apply to notices served by the water authority. Particulars of notices served under this section must be entered in the register maintained by the water authority under s. 41: see sub-s. (4) and (5).

SUB-S. (1)

"First mentioned": this presumably refers to an entry alleged to be attributable to an act or omission which is in accordance with "good agricultural practice". The Secretary of State must then serve a notice on the occupier, but this may be less restrictive than the request from the water authority (sub-s. (3)), and the notice may subsequently be cancelled (sub-s. (4)).

52. Charges in respect of certain discharges in England and Wales

(1) The Secretary of State may, by an order made after consultation with the National Water Council, provide that sections 30 and 31 of the Water Act 1973 (which among other things relate to charges for facilities provided by water authorities and to schemes for the payment of the charges) shall apply to discharges of trade or sewage effluent which are made or authorised to be made by virtue of a consent given in pursuance of this Act or the Public Health (Drainage of Trade Premises) Act 1937 as those sections apply to facilities provided by water authorities; and any such order may—

(*a*) provide that, in the said section 30 as applied by the order, subsection (4) (under which regard is to be had to the cost of providing facilities in fixing charges for the facilities) and references to that subsection shall be omitted; and

(*b*) repeal sections 59 (1) (*e*) and 61 (4) of the Public Health Act 1961 (which provide for conditions relating to charges to be attached to consents for discharges which are given in pursuance of the said Act of 1937).

(2) An order made in pursuance of the preceding subsection—

(*a*) shall include provision for appeals to the Secretary of State in respect of charges payable to a water authority by virtue of that subsection; and

(*b*) may include provision for the giving by the Secretary of State in consequence of an appeal of directions in respect of the charges to the authority or any other party to the appeal (including directions as to the charges which are to be payable in respect of any period before the determination of the appeal);

and the Secretary of State may by order vary or revoke any provisions which by virtue of this subsection or section 104 (1) (*a*) of this Act are contained in an order made in pursuance of this section.

(3) This section does not apply to Scotland. [**81**]

DEFINITIONS

National Water Council:	This is the successor to the Water Resources Board, established by the Water Act 1973, s. 4.
Order:	made under s. 105 (1)
Sewage effluent:	s. 56 (1)
Trade effluent:	s. 105 (1)
Water authority:	Water Act 1973, s. 2

GENERAL NOTE

This section empowers the Secretary of State to make an order fixing rates of charges for facilities provided by water authorities for the discharge of sewage or trade effluent into public sewers from trade premises. Any such order will *not* be subject to the negative resolution procedure: s. 104 (1).

53. [*Applies to Scotland only.*]

54. Exclusion of certain liability in respect of discharges, etc., with consent

Any entry of matter into a stream or controlled waters which—

(*a*) is authorised by a consent given in pursuance of this Part of this Act and is in accordance with the conditions (if any) to which the consent is subject; or

(*b*) is a consequence of an act which is so authorised and in accordance with such conditions;

shall not constitute an offence under section 8 of the Salmon and Freshwater Fisheries Act 1923 or section 68 of the Public Health Act 1875. [**82**]

DEFINITIONS

Sewage effluent:	s. 56 (1)
Stream:	s. 56 (1) and s. 56 (3)
Trade effluent:	s. 105 (1)

GENERAL NOTE

Conditions of a kind prescribed by regulations made under s. 36 (8) are to be disregarded for this purpose.

Supplemental

55. Discharges by water authorities

(1) This Part of this Act shall have effect with prescribed modifications in relation to discharges by a water authority in its area.

(2) Without prejudice to the generality of the power to make regulations conferred by the preceding subsection, any regulations made in pursuance of that subsection may provide for consents required by water authorities for the purposes of this Part of this Act as modified by virtue of that subsection to be or be deemed to be given by the Secretary of State.

(3) [*Applies to Scotland only.*] [**83**]

DEFINITIONS

Area:	s. 56 (4)
Prescribed:	by regulations: s. 105 (1)
Regulations:	made by the Secretary of State: s. 105 (1)
Water authority:	Water Act 1973, s. 2

GENERAL NOTE

This section makes it clear that, subject to any modifications prescribed by regulations, the controls of Part II will apply to discharges made by a water authority in its own area. Discharges by an authority into the area of another water authority will also be subject to Part II, presumably without modification.

56. Interpretation, etc., of Part II.

(1) Except where the context otherwise requires, in this Part of this Act—

"controlled waters" means the sea within three nautical miles from any point on the coast measured from low-water mark of ordinary spring tides, such other parts of the territorial sea adjacent to Great Britain as are prescribed and any other tidal waters in Great Britain;

"relevant waters" has the meaning assigned to it by section 31 (1) (*a*) of this Act;

"restricted waters" means controlled waters in—

(*a*) areas designated by regulations as tidal rivers for the purposes of this definition; and

(*b*) other areas of a kind prescribed for the purposes of this definition as areas in which, in the opinion of the Secretary of State, vessels commonly lie at moorings in close proximity to one another;

"sewage effluent" includes any effluent from the sewage disposal or sewerage works of a water authority;

"specified underground water" means underground water in the area of a water authority which is specified, as water which is used or is expected by the authority to be used for any purpose, in a document which is in a form prescribed for the purposes of this definition and contains prescribed particulars and of which a copy is kept available, and has for not less than one month been kept available, at the principal office of the authority for inspection by the public free of charge during office hours;

"stream" includes any river, watercourse or inland water, whether the river, watercourse or inland water is natural or artificial or above or below ground, except—

(*a*) subject to subsection (3) of this section, any lake, loch or pond which does not discharge into a stream;

(*b*) any sewer vested in a water authority; and

(*c*) any tidal waters;

and any reference to a stream includes a reference to the channel or bed of a stream which is for the time being dry; and

"tidal waters" includes the waters of any enclosed dock which adjoins tidal waters.

(2) [*Applies to Scotland only.*]

(3) Regulations may provide that any prescribed lake, loch or pond which does not discharge into a stream, or that any lake, loch or pond of a prescribed description which does not discharge into a stream, shall be a stream for the purposes of this Part of this Act.

(4) For the purposes of this Part of this Act the area of a water authority shall include all controlled waters off the coast of the area which is the authority's area apart from this subsection; and any question as to whether any place is included in the area of a water authority by virtue of this subsection shall be determined by the Secretary of State.

(5) For the purposes of this Part of this Act a notice imposing conditions with respect to discharges which was given by an authority in pursuance of—

(*a*) section 7 (4) of the Rivers (Prevention of Pollution) Act 1951; or

(*b*) [*applies to Scotland only*];

(*c*) section 1 (5) of the Rivers (Prevention of Pollution) Act 1961; or

(*d*) [*applies to Scotland only*]

shall be treated as having given the authority's consent in pursuance of the Act in question for those discharges subject to those conditions.

(6) Section 30 (5) of this Act shall have effect in relation to this Part of this Act as if for any reference to Part I of this Act there were substituted a reference to this Part of this Act. **[84]**

DEFINITIONS

Prescribed:	by regulations made by the Secretary of State: s. 105 (1)
Water authority:	Water Act 1973, s. 2

SUB-S. (1)

The public will be able readily to ascertain *which* underground waters are "specified" for the purposes of Part II. For a definition of "trade effluent", see s. 105 (1).

SUB-S. (3)

Note that regulations may, in effect, extend the definition of "stream" in a particular case.

SUB-S. (4)

"Controlled waters": see sub-s. (1).

Part III
Noise

INTRODUCTION TO PART III

[85] Unlike Part II, which builds on and strengthens existing statutory controls, Part III makes virtually a fresh start so as to deal with noise control. The Noise Abatement Act 1960 is repealed by Sch. 4, but the provisions of s. 1 of that Act enabling a noise nuisance to be dealt with as a statutory nuisance under the Public Health Act 1936, is replaced by s. 58, enabling a local authority (a district council, a London Borough Council, the Common Council of the City, and the two Temples: s. 73 (1)[1]) to take summary proceedings in respect of noise amounting to a nuisance; under s. 59 a complaint of such a nuisance may also be made by an aggrieved occupier of premises. Statutory undertakers are no longer immune from proceedings of this kind. The other subject dealt with by the Act of 1960, noise in streets, is now covered in similar terms by s. 62. The remaining provisions of Part III are quite new. Sections 60 and 61 deal with construction sites. The local authority may serve a notice on any person carrying out construction works, imposing requirements (in particular so as to ensure that the "best practicable means"—see s. 72—are employed to minimise noise) as to how the works are to be carried out (s. 60). Alternatively, a person intending to carry out construction works may apply to the local authority for a consent under s. 61, and in granting consent the authority may impose conditions in any such consent. An appeal lies to the magistrates against a refusal of consent or conditions imposed in a consent (s. 61 (7)) or against a notice under s. 60 (s. 60 (7)), but if the work is carried out in accordance with a consent the person carrying out the work will have a defence in any summary proceedings taken under s. 59 by an occupier of premises.

[86] Sections 63–67 with ss. 69 and 70, and Sch. I, are concerned with the novel device of noise abatement zones. An order designating a zone ("a noise abatement order") will apply to the whole or any part of the area of a local authority, and it will

[1] But *not* a port health authority: s. 73 (4).

specify the classes of premises to which it will apply. When an order has been made by the local authority declaring a noise abatement zone, publicity must be given in accordance with paras. 1 and 2 of Sch. I, and if objections are made, the Secretary of State must hold a local inquiry before confirming the order; the order will not come into effect unless and until it has been so confirmed (s. 63). As soon as may be after the making of an order the local authority must measure the level of noise emanating from any premises within the zone and record these in a "noise level register" (which is to be open to public inspection); notice of the level so recorded must be served on the owner and occupier of premises concerned, who will have the right to appeal against the record to the Secretary of State (s. 64). It is then made an offence for the noise level so recorded to be exceeded, except with the consent of the local authority, and there is a right of appeal to the Secretary of State against a refusal of such consent (s. 65). Under s. 66 the local authority may, by serving a "noise reduction order" in respect of premises subject to a noise abatement order, require the level of noise emanating from specified premises to be reduced as may be therein specified: there is a right of appeal to the local magistrates against such a notice. Section 67 empowers the local authority to determine the acceptable level of noise in the case of a proposed new building, which when constructed, will be subject to a noise abatement order. An appeal lies to the Secretary of State against any such determination.

[**87**] Default powers in the case of failure to carry out works so as to comply with a noise abatement notice, a noise reduction notice, or an order of the court under this Part, are given to the local authority by s. 69; and s. 70 regulates the procedure for appeals under Part III. Section 68 empowers the Secretary of State to make regulations for the reduction of noise caused by plant or machinery, whether or not within a noise abatement zone.

[**88**] Section 73 is concerned with definitions, and s. 74 with penalties for offences under Part III. "Noise" in Part III, it should be noted, expressly does *not* include aircraft noise: s. 73 (3), but it does include vibration.

Periodical inspections by local authorities

57. Periodical inspections by local authorities

It shall be the duty of every local authority to cause its area to be inspected from time to time—

(*a*) to detect anything which ought to be dealt with under the following section; and

(*b*) to decide how to exercise its powers concerning noise abatement zones.

[89]

DEFINITIONS

Local authority: s. 73 (1)
Noise abatement zone: s. 73 (1) and s. 63

GENERAL NOTE

This duty of the local authority to inspect their area from time to time is similar to the duties of housing authorities under the Housing Act 1957. It is enforceable by the default powers of the Secretary of State under s. 97.

Summary proceedings to deal with noise

58. Summary proceedings by local authorities

(1) Where a local authority is satisfied that noise amounting to a nuisance

exists, or is likely to occur or recur, in the area of the local authority, the local authority shall serve a notice imposing all or any of the following requirements—

(*a*) requiring the abatement of the nuisance or prohibiting or restricting its occurrence or recurrence;

(*b*) requiring the execution of such works, and the taking of such other steps, as may be necessary for the purpose of the notice or as may be specified in the notice;

and the notice shall specify the time or times within which the requirements of the notice are to be complied with.

(2) The notice shall be served on the person responsible for the nuisance or, if that person cannot be found or the nuisance has not yet occurred, on the owner or occupier of the premises from which the noise is emitted or would be emitted.

(3) The person served with the notice may appeal against the notice to a magistrates' court within twenty-one days from service of the notice.

(4) If a person on whom a notice is served under this section without reasonable excuse contravenes any requirement of the notice, he shall be guilty of an offence against this Part of this Act.

(5) In proceedings for an offence under the preceding subsection in respect of noise caused in the course of a trade or business, it shall be a defence to prove that the best practicable means have been used for preventing, or for counteracting the effect of, the noise.

(6) In proceedings for an offence under subsection (4) of this section of contravening requirements imposed by virtue of subsection (1) (*a*) of this section it shall be a defence to prove—

(*a*) that the alleged offence was covered by a notice served under section 60 or a consent given under section 61 or 65 of this Act; or

(*b*) where the alleged offence was committed at a time when the premises were subject to a notice under section 66 of this Act, that the level of noise emanating from the premises at that time was not such as to constitute a contravention of the notice under section 66; or

(*c*) where the alleged offence was committed at a time when the premises were not subject to a notice under section 66 of this Act, and when a level fixed under section 67 of this Act applied to the premises, that the level of noise emanating from the premises at that time did not exceed that level.

Paragraphs (*b*) and (*c*) above apply whether or not the relevant notice was subject to appeal at the time when the offence was alleged to have been committed.

(7) Where a nuisance which exists or has occurred within the area of a local authority, or which has affected any part of that area, appears to the local authority to be wholly or partly caused by some act or default committed or taking place outside its area, the local authority may act under this section as if the act or default were wholly within that area, except that any appeal shall be heard by a magistrates' court having jurisdiction where the act or default is alleged to have taken place.

(8) If a local authority is of opinion that proceedings for an offence under subsection (4) of this section would afford an inadequate remedy in the case of any noise which is a nuisance, they may take proceedings in the High Court or, in Scotland, in any court of competent jurisdiction for the purpose of securing

the abatement, prohibition or restriction of the nuisance, and the proceedings shall be maintainable notwithstanding that the local authority has suffered no damage from the nuisance; but in any proceedings taken in pursuance of this subsection it shall be a defence to prove that the noise was authorised by a notice under section 60 or a consent under section 61 of this Act.

(9) Section 1 of the Noise Abatement Act 1960 (which is superseded by this section) shall cease to have effect except as respects notices served by virtue of that section before the coming into force of this section. [**90**]

DEFINITIONS

Best practicable means:	s. 72
Contravenes:	s. 73 (1)
Local authority:	s. 73 (1)
Offence:	s. 74
Person responsible:	s. 73 (1)
Premises:	s. 105 (1)

GENERAL NOTE

This section replaces s. 1 of the Noise Abatement Act 1960 (repealed by Sch. 4, subject to sub-s. (9)) and provides for summary proceedings to be taken at the instance of the local authority in the case of noise or vibrations which amounts to a nuisance. In the 1960 Act such noise was to be treated as a statutory nuisance for the purposes of the Public Health Act 1936, but this notion has now been abandoned. "Noise" includes vibration (s. 73 (1)), and it seems that nuisance must be understood in its common law sense, in that it must unduly interfere with the comfortable and convenient enjoyment by a neighbour of his land (see *Thompson-Schwab* v. *Costaki*, [1956] 1 All E.R. 652, cited in Clerk & Lindsell on *Torts* (13th edn., at p. 782)). Examples of cases involving nuisance by noise or vibrations include *Soltau* v. *De Held* (1851) 2 Sim.N.S. 133 (bell-ringing), *Vanderplant* v. *Mayfair Hotel Co. Ltd.*,, [1930] 1 Ch. 138 (early morning clatter from a kitchen), *Lebor* v. *Trans-World Airline* (1953), 215 L.T.Jo. 116, and *Halsey* v. *Esso Petroleum Co., Ltd.*, [1961] 2 All E.R. 145, and see Clerk & Lindsell, *op. cit.* As to proceedings taken by a private individual, see s. 59.

Note that this section may be used before a noise nuisance has actually occurred and also it may be used if such a nuisance is likely to recur, thereby (in the latter instance) making irrelevant in this context the procedure of the Public Health (Recurring Nuisances) Act 1969.

It also seems that "nuisance" in this section, and in s. 54, connotes a private nuisance, and that it is not necessary to establish a public nuisance. If there is no *public* element in the nuisance whatever, the local authority may consider it preferable for proceedings to be taken by the complainant under s. 59.

SUB-S. (1)

The notice, which should be served in accordance with s. 233 of the Local Government Act 1972, need not specify works or the steps required to be taken, but may do so. A reasonable time limit should be given for compliance.

SUB-S. (3)

As to appeals, see s. 70.

SUB-S. (4)

"Reasonable excuse" is not defined, but see the defence afforded by sub-ss. (5) and (6).

SUB-S. (6)

Sections 60 and 61 refer to construction sites, and ss. 65, 66 and 67 are concerned with action taken in relation to noise abatement zones.

SUB-S. (8)

Compare Public Health Act 1936, s. 100.

59. Summary proceedings by occupier of premises

(1) A magistrates' court may act under this section on a complaint made by the occupier of any premises on the ground that in his capacity as occupier of the premises he is aggrieved by noise amounting to a nuisance.

(2) If the magistrates' court is satisfied that the alleged nuisance exists, or that although abated it is likely to recur on the same premises, the court shall make an order for either or both of the following purposes—

(*a*) requiring the defendant to abate the nuisance, within a time specified in the order and to execute any works necessary for that purpose;

(*b*) prohibiting a recurrence of the nuisance, and requiring the defendant, within a time specified in the order, to execute any works necessary to prevent the recurrence.

(3) Proceedings under this section shall be brought against the person responsible for the nuisance or, if that person cannot be found, against the owner or occupier of the premises from which the noise is emitted or would be emitted.

(4) A person who without reasonable excuse contravenes any requirement of an order under subsection (2) of this section shall be guilty of an offence against this Part of this Act.

(5) In proceedings for an offence under this section in respect of noise caused in the course of a trade or business, it shall be a defence to prove that the best practicable means have been used for preventing, or for counteracting the effect of, the noise.

(6) If a person is convicted of an offence under subsection (4) of this section, a magistrates' court may, after giving the local authority in whose area the nuisance has occurred an opportunity of being heard, direct the authority to do anything which the person convicted was required to do by the order to which the conviction relates.

(7) [*Applies to Scotland only.*] **[91]**

DEFINITIONS

Best practicable means:	s. 72
Contravenes:	s. 73 (1)
Local authority:	s. 73 (1)
Noise:	s. 73 (1) and s. 73 (3)
Offence:	s. 74
Person responsible:	s. 73 (1)
Premises:	s. 105 (1)

GENERAL NOTE

This section is in many respects a repetition of s. 58, but the important difference is that proceedings for the abatement of a noise nuisance may be commenced before the magistrates by a single individual occupier of premises, who is aggrieved by the noise. For other comments, see s. 58. Under the 1960 Act there had to be *three* complainants.

SUB-S. (1)

"Person aggrieved": the plaintiff, or prosecutor, in such proceedings must be able to show that the noise is causing a nuisance to *him*. There is now considerable case law on the meaning of "person aggrieved" (see, for example, *A.-G.- of Gambia* v. *N'Jie*, [1961] A.C. 617; [1961] 2 All E.R. 504), but these would seem not to be relevant to the present context. A mere busybody is in any event unlikely to be an occupier. This subsection can be used only in respect of an *actual* nuisance, and not in anticipation of one that it is likely will occur.

Construction sites

60. Control of noise on construction sites

(1) This section applies to works of the following description, that is to say—

(*a*) the erection, construction, alteration, repair or maintenance of buildings, structures or roads;
(*b*) breaking up, opening or boring under any road or adjacent land in connection with the construction, inspection, maintenance or removal of works;
(*c*) demolition or dredging work; and
(*d*) (whether or not also comprised in paragraph (*a*), (*b*) or (*c*) above) any work of engineering construction.

(2) Where it appears to a local authority that works to which this section applies are being, or are going to be, carried out on any premises, the local authority may serve a notice imposing requirements as to the way in which the works are to be carried out and may if it thinks fit publish notice of the requirements as to the way in which the works are to be appropriate.

(3) The notice may in particular—

(*a*) specify the plant or machinery which is or is not to be used;
(*b*) specify the hours during which the works may be carried out;
(*c*) specify the level of noise which may be emitted from the premises in question or at any specified point on those premises or which may be so emitted during specified hours; and
(*d*) provide for any change of circumstances.

(4) In acting under this section the local authority shall have regard—

(*a*) to the relevant provisions of any code of practice issued under this Part of this Act;
(*b*) to the need for ensuring that the best practicable means are employed to minimise noise;
(*c*) before specifying any particular methods or plant or machinery, to the desirability in the interests of any recipients of the notice in question of specifying other methods or plant or machinery which would be substantially as effective in minimising noise and more acceptable to them;
(*d*) to the need to protect any persons in the locality in which the premises in question are situated from the effects of noise.

(5) A notice under this section shall be served on the person who appears to the local authority to be carrying out, or going to carry out, the works, and on such other persons appearing to the local authority to be responsible for, or to have control over, the carrying out of the works as the local authority thinks fit.

(6) A notice under this section may specify the time within which the notice is to be complied with, and may require the execution of such works, and the taking of such other steps, as may be necessary for the purpose of the notice, or as may be specified in the notice.

(7) A person served with a notice under this section may appeal against the notice to a magistrates' court within twenty-one days from the service of the notice.

(8) If a person on whom a notice is served under this section without reasonable excuse contravenes any requirement of the notice he shall be guilty of an offence against this Part of this Act. [**92**]

DEFINITIONS

Best practicable means:	s. 72
Contravenes:	s. 73 (1)
Local authority:	s. 73 (1)
Noise:	s. 73 (1) and s. 73 (3)
Offence:	s. 74
Person responsible:	s. 73 (1)
Work of engineering construction:	s. 73 (1)

GENERAL NOTE

This section, and s. 61 deal, for the first time in legislative history, with the particular problem of noise on construction sites. Under this section the local authority take the initiative and serve a notice specifying how the works are to be carried out; under s. 62 a person intending to carry out works may apply in advance for a consent as to the methods by which the works are to be carried out. Compliance with the terms of a notice or a consent does not of itself provide a defence to nuisance abatement proceedings under either s. 58 or s. 59, and indeed in the case of consents this is expressly provided for so far as proceedings by a private individual under s. 59 are concerned (see s. 61 (9)).

SUB-S. (2)

Service of notices should be effected in accordance with s. 233 of the Local Government Act 1972.

SUB-S. (4)

As to codes of practice, see s. 71.

SUB-S. (7)

As to appeals, see s. 70.

61. Prior consent for work on construction sites

(1) A person who intends to carry out works to which the preceding section applies may apply to the local authority for a consent under this section.

(2) Where approval under building regulations under Part II of the Public Health Act 1936, or in Scotland a warrant under section 6 of the Building (Scotland) Act 1959, is required for the carrying out of the works, the application under this section must be made at the same time as, or later than, the request for the approval under building regulations or, as the case may be, the application for a warrant under the said Act of 1959.

(3) An application under this section shall contain particulars of—

(*a*) the works, and the method by which they are to be carried out; and (*b*) the steps proposed to be taken to minimise noise resulting from the works.

(4) If the local authority considers that the application contains sufficient information for the purpose and that, if the works are carried out in accordance with the application, it would not serve a notice under the preceding section in respect of those works, the local authority shall give its consent to the application.

(5) In acting under this section a local authority shall have regard to the considerations set out in subsection (4) of the preceding section and shall have power to—

(*a*) attach any conditions to a consent; and
(*b*) limit or qualify a consent to allow for any change in circumstances; and
(*c*) limit the duration of a consent;

and any person who knowingly carries out the works, or permits the works to be carried out, in contravention of any conditions attached to a consent under this section shall be guilty of an offence against this Part of this Act.

(6) The local authority shall inform the applicant of its decision on the application within twenty-eight days from receipt of the application; and if the local authority gives its consent to the application it may if it thinks fit publish notice of the consent, and of the works to which it relates, in such way as appears to the local authority to be appropriate.

(7) If—

(*a*) the local authority does not give a consent within the said period of twenty-eight days; or
(*b*) the local authority gives its consent within the said period of twenty-eight days but attaches any condition to the consent or limits or qualifies the consent in any way,

the applicant may appeal to a magistrates' court within twenty-one days from the end of that period.

(8) In any proceedings for an offence under section 60 (8) of this Act it shall be a defence to prove that the alleged contravention amounted to the carrying out of the works in accordance with a consent given under this section.

(9) A consent given under this section shall contain a statement to the effect that the consent does not of itself constitute any ground of defence against any proceedings instituted under section 59 of this Act.

(10) Where a consent has been given under this section and the works are carried out by a person other than the applicant for the consent, it shall be the duty of the applicant to take all reasonable steps to bring the consent to the notice of that other person; and if he fails to comply with this subsection he shall be guilty of an offence against this Part of this Act. [**93**]

DEFINITIONS

Contravention:	s. 73 (1)
Local authority:	s. 73 (1)
Noise:	s. 73 (1) and s. 73 (3)
Offence:	s. 74

GENERAL NOTE

See General Note to s. 60.

SUB-S. (1)

No form has been prescribed for such applications, but they should presumably be made in writing. "Sufficient information" must be given (see sub-s. (4)), and see also sub-s. (3).

SUB-S. (2)

Approval under building regulations is normally required when any person intends to erect a building, make any structural alteration of or extension to a building, execute any works or install any fitting in connection with a building, or make any material change of use of a building (Buildings Regulations 1972, S.I. 1972 No. 317, reg. A.10).

SUB-S. (7)

Appeals: see s. 70.

Noise in streets

62. Noise in streets

(1) Subject to the provisions of this section, a loud-speaker in a street shall not be operated—

(*a*) between the hours of nine in the evening and eight in the following morning, for any purpose;

(*b*) at any other time, for the purpose of advertising any entertainment, trade or business;

and any person who operates or permits the operation of a loudspeaker in contravention of this subsection shall be guilty of an offence against this Part of this Act.

In this subsection "street" means a highway and any other road, footway, square or court which is for the time being open to the public.

(2) The preceding subsection shall not apply to the operation of a loudspeaker—

(*a*) for police, fire brigade or ambulance purposes, by a water authority in the exercise of any of its functions, or by a local authority within its area;

(*b*) for communicating with persons on a vessel for the purpose of directing the movement of that or any other vessel;

(*c*) if the loudspeaker forms part of a public telephone system;

(*d*) if the loudspeaker—

(i) is in or fixed to a vehicle, and

(ii) is operated solely for the entertainment of or for communicating with the driver or a passenger of the vehicle or, where the loudspeaker is or forms part of the horn or similar warning instrument of the vehicle, solely for giving warning to other traffic, and

(iii) is so operated as not to give reasonable cause for annoyance to persons in the vicinity;

(*e*) otherwise than on a highway, by persons employed in connection with a transport undertaking used by the public in a case where the loudspeaker is operated solely for making announcements to passengers or prospective passengers or to other persons so employed;

(*f*) by a travelling showman on land which is being used for the purposes of a pleasure fair;

(*g*) in case of emergency.

(3) Subsection (1) (*b*) of this section shall not apply to the operation of a loudspeaker between the hours of noon and seven in the evening on the same day if the loudspeaker—

(*a*) is fixed to a vehicle which is being used for the conveyance of a perishable commodity for human consumption; and

(*b*) is operated solely for informing members of the public (otherwise than by means of words) that the commodity is on sale from the vehicle; and

(*c*) is so operated as not to give reasonable cause for annoyance to persons in the vicinity.

(4) [*Applies to Scotland only.*] **[94]**

DEFINITIONS

Contravention:	s. 73 (1)
Local authority:	s. 73 (1)
Offence:	s. 74
Street:	sub-s. (1)
Water authority:	see Water Act 1974, s. 2

GENERAL NOTE

This section amounts to a re-enactment of s. 2 of the Noise Abatement Act 1960, except that the definition of "loudspeaker" in s. 2 (5) of that Act, so as to include "a megaphone and any other device for amplifying sound", has not been repeated.

Noise abatement zones

63. Designation of zones

(1) A local authority may by order confirmed by the Secretary of State designate all or any part of its area a noise abatement zone.

(2) An order under this section shall specify the classes of premises to which it applies (that is to say, the classes of premises subject to control under the following provisions of this Part of this Act).

(3) An order made and confirmed under this section may be revoked or varied by a subsequent order so made and confirmed.

(4) The provisions of Schedule 1 to this Act shall apply to the confirmation and coming into operation of an order under this section.

(5) In this Part of this Act a "noise abatement order" means an order made under this section. **[95]**

DEFINITION

Local authority: s. 73 (1)

GENERAL NOTE

As to comment on noise abatement zones, see Introduction to this Part. For the procedure on the making of an order, see Sch. 1 and s. 104 (1).

64. Register of noise levels

(1) Every local authority which has designated its area or any part of its area a noise abatement zone shall measure the level of noise emanating from premises within the zone which are of any class to which the relevant noise abatement order relates.

(2) The local authority shall record all measurements taken in pursuance of the preceding subsection in a register (in this Part of this Act referered to as a "noise level register") to be kept by the local authority for the purpose in accordance with regulations.

(3) The local authority on recording any measurement in the noise level register shall serve a copy of that record on the owner and occupier of the premises in respect of which the measurement was taken; and any person on whom a copy of such a record is served may, within twenty-eight days of the date of service, appeal to the Secretary of State against the record.

(4) On an appeal to the Secretary of State in pursuance of the preceding subsection the Secretary of State may give to the local authority in question such directions as he thinks fit as to the record of the measurement of noise which is the subject of the appeal, and it shall be the duty of the authority to comply with the directions.

(5) Except as provided by the preceding provisions of this section the validity or accuracy of any entry in a noise level register shall not be questioned in any proceedings under this Part of this Act.

(6) The premises as to which a local authority is to make measurements under this section shall include those which come within a class to which the relevant noise abatement order relates after the making of the order; and it shall be for the local authority to determine, both for those premises and all other premises of any class to which the relevant noise abatement order relates, where the measurements under this section are to be made.

(7) A noise level register shall be open to public inspection at the principal office of the local authority free of charge at all reasonable hours, and the local authority shall afford members of the public reasonable facilities for obtaining from the authority, on payment of reasonable charges, copies of entries in the register.

(8) Provision may be made by regulations—

(*a*) for determining, or for authorising the Secretary of State to determine, the methods by which noise levels are to be measured for the purposes of any provision of this section and the three following sections; and

(*b*) for enabling noise levels calculated in accordance with the regulations, or in accordance with the directions of the Secretary of State, to be treated for those purposes as measured by a method determined in pursuance of the preceding paragraph. [**96**]

DEFINITIONS

Local authority:	s. 73 (1)
Noise:	s. 73 (1) and s. 73 (3)
Noise abatement order:	s. 63 (5)
Noise abatement zone:	s. 63 (1)
Noise level register:	sub-s. (2)
Offence:	s. 74
Owner:	s. 105 (1)
Premises:	s. 105 (1)
Regulations:	made by the Secretary of State: s. 105 (1)

GENERAL NOTE

This section sets out the first consequences of the making of a noise abatement order. The local authority must, as soon as practicable after the making of the order, (but see sub-s. (6)) record the level of noise emanating from premises within the zone which are of a class to which the order relates. They will then subsequently be able, if they see fit, to serve a noise reduction notice under s. 66, or they may have to consider applications for consent to an increase in the level of noise under s. 65. It will presumably be their responsibility to monitor classified premises from time to time and ensure that the noise level recorded in the register is not exceeded, in contravention of s. 65 (1).

SUB-S. (3)

The copy of the record should be served in accordance with s. 233 of the Local Government Act 1972. As to appeals, see s. 70 (2).

SUB-S. (5)

This provision excludes the jurisdiction of the courts to question the validity of an entry, and in particular, the noise level so recorded will not be open to question in proceedings under s. 65 (1) and (5).

65. Noise exceeding registered level

(1) The level of noise recorded in the noise level register in respect of any premises shall not be exceeded except with the consent in writing of the local authority.

(2) The local authority's consent may be made subject to such conditions, whether as to the amount by which the level of noise may be increased, or as to the period for which, or the periods during which, the level of noise may be increased, as may be specified in the consent; and the authority shall record particulars of the consent in the noise level register.

(3) If within the period of two months beginning with the date on which a local authority receives an application for its consent under this section, or within such longer period as the authority and the applicant agree in writing, the authority has not notified the applicant of its decision on the application, the authority shall be deemed to have refused consent in pursuance of the application.

(4) An applicant for consent under this section may appeal to the Secretary of State against the local authority's decision on the application within the period of three months beginning with the date on which the authority notifies him of the decision or, in a case falling within the preceding subsection, beginning with the expiration of the period or longer period there mentioned; and it shall be the duty of the local authority to act in accordance with the decision of the Secretary of State on the appeal.

(5) If noise emitted from any premises constitutes a contravention of subsection (1) of this section or of a condition attached to a consent under this section, the person responsible shall be guilty of an offence against this Part of this Act.

(6) The magistrates' court convicting a person of an offence under the preceding subsection may, if satisfied that the offence is likely to continue or recur, make an order requiring the execution of any works necessary to prevent it continuing or recurring; and if that person without reasonable excuse contravenes any requirement of the order he shall be guilty of an offence against this Part of this Act.

(7) The magistrates' court may, after giving the local authority in whose area

the premises are situated an opportunity of being heard, direct the local authority to do anything which the court has power under the preceding subsection to require the person convicted to do, either instead of, or in addition to, imposing any requirement on that person.

(8) A consent given under this section shall contain a statement to the effect that the consent does not of itself constitute any ground of defence against any proceedings instituted under section 59 of this Act. **[97]**

DEFINITIONS

Contravenes, contravention:	s. 73 (1)
Local authority:	s. 73 (1)
Noise:	s. 73 (1) and s. 73 (3)
Noise level register:	s. 64 (2)
Person responsible:	s. 73 (1)
Premises:	s. 105 (1)

GENERAL NOTE

This section starts by creating the substantive offence of exceeding the registered noise level, and then makes provision for applications to be made for the consent of the local authority to an increase in that level. This can of course apply only to premises within a noise abatement zone, to which the noise abatement order applies.

SUB-S. (1)

Should be read with sub-s. (5).

SUB-S. (2)

Note the limitation on the kinds of conditions that may be specified in a consent.

SUB-S. (4)

As to appeals, see s. 70.

SUB-S. (6)

As to orders under this subsection, see s. 104 (1).

66. Reduction of noise levels

(1) If it appears to the local authority—

(*a*) that the level of noise emanating from any premises to which a noise abatement order applies is not acceptable having regard to the purposes for which the order was made; and

(*b*) that a reduction in that level is practicable at reasonable cost and would afford a public benefit,

the local authority may serve a notice on the person responsible.

(2) The notice shall require that person—

(*a*) to reduce the level of noise emanating from the premises to such level as may be specified in the notice;

(*b*) to prevent any subsequent increase in the level of noise emanating from those premises without the consent of the local authority; and

(*c*) to take such steps as may be specified in the notice to achieve those purposes.

(3) A notice under this section (in this Part of this Act referred to as a "noise reduction notice") shall specify a time, not being less than six months

from the date of service of the notice, within which the noise level is to be reduced to the specified level and, where the notice specifies any steps necessary to achieve that purpose, within which those steps shall be taken.

(4) A noise reduction notice may specify particular times, or particular days, during which the noise level is to be reduced, and may require the noise level to be reduced to different levels for different times or days.

(5) A notice under this section shall take effect whether or not a consent under the preceding section authorises a level of noise higher than that specified in the notice.

(6) The local authority shall record particulars of a noise reduction notice in the noise level register.

(7) A person who is served with a noise reduction notice may, within three months of the date of service, appeal to a magistrates' court against the notice.

(8) A person who without reasonable excuse contravenes a noise reduction notice shall be guilty of an offence against this Part of this Act.

(9) In proceedings for an offence under the preceding subsection in respect of noise caused in the course of a trade or business, it shall be a defence to prove that the best practicable means had been used for preventing, or for counteracting the effect of, the noise. [**98**]

DEFINITIONS

Best practicable means:	s. 72
Contravenes:	s. 73 (1)
Local authority:	s. 73 (1)
Noise:	s. 73 (1) and s. 73 (3)
Noise abatement order:	s. 63 (5)
Noise level register:	s. 64 (2)
Noise reduction notice:	sub-s. (3)
Offence:	s. 74
Person responsible:	s. 73 (1) and s. 73 (3)
Premises:	s. 105 (1)

GENERAL NOTE

This is the section that enables a local authority to secure a reduction in the recorded noise level from classified premises within a noise abatement zone. In order to achieve this, it must be shown that the level of noise is not acceptable, that reduction is practicable at reasonable expense, and that it would afford a *public* benefit. Such a notice must override the terms of a consent given under s. 65 (sub-s. (5)). This section (with modifications) may be applied to a new building—see s. 67 (5).

SUB-S. (1)

Service should be effected in accordance with s. 233 of the Local Government Act 1972.

SUB-S. (7)

As to appeals, see s. 70.

67. New buildings, etc.

(1) Where it appears to the local authority—

(*a*) that a building is going to be constructed and that a noise abatement order will apply to it when it is erected; or (*b*) that any premises will, as the result of any works, become premises to which a noise abatement order applies,

the local authority may, on the application of the owner or occupier of the premises or a person who satisfies the authority that he is negotiating to acquire an interest in the premises or on its own initiative, determine the level of noise which will be acceptable as that emanating from the premises.

(2) The local authority shall record in the noise level register the level of noise determined under this section for any premises.

(3) The local authority shall give notice of its intention to the applicant or, in the case of a decision made on its own initiative, to the owner or the occupier of the premises, and the recipient of the notice may appeal to the Secretary of State against that decision within three months of the date on which the local authority notifies him of that decision; and it shall be the duty of the local authority to act in accordance with the decision of the Secretary of State on the appeal.

(4) If within the period of two months beginning with the date when the local authority receives an application in pursuance of subsection (1) of this section, the authority has not given notice to the applicant of its decision on the application, the authority shall be deemed to have given him notice on the expiration of that period that it has decided not to make a determination in pursuance of the application; and the applicant may accordingly appeal against the decision to the Secretary of State in pursuance of the preceding subsection.

(5) Where at any time after the coming into force of a noise abatement order any premises become premises to which the order applies as a result of the construction of a building or as a result of any works carried out on the premises but no level of noise has been determined under this section as respects the premises, section 66 of this Act shall apply as if—

(*a*) paragraph (*b*) of subsection (1) were omitted; and
(*b*) three months were substituted for six months in subsection (3); and
(*c*) subsection (9) were omitted. **[99]**

DEFINITIONS

Local authority:	s. 73 (1)
Noise:	s. 73 (1) and s. 73 (3)
Noise abatement order:	s. 63 (5)
Noise level register:	s. 64 (2)
Owner:	s. 105 (1)
Premises:	s. 105 (1)

GENERAL NOTE

This section enables a local authority to determine the level of acceptable noise for a new or other building which, when erected or altered, will be subject to a noise abatement order. This may be done on the application of the owner, occupier or prospective owner, or on the initiative of the authority.

SUB-S. (1)

There is no prescribed form for such an application.

SUB-S. (3)

Service of the notice should be effected in accordance with s. 233 of the Local Government Act 1972. As to appeals, see s. 70.

Noise from plant or machinery

68. Noise from plant or machinery

(1) Provision may be made by regulations—

(*a*) for requiring the use on or in connection with any plant or machinery of devices or arrangements for reducing the noise caused by the plant or machinery;

(*b*) for limiting the level of noise which may be caused by any plant or machinery when used for works to which section 60 of this Act applies or which may be caused outside a factory within the meaning of the Factories Act 1961 by the use of plant or machinery in the factory;

and regulations under this section may apply standards, specifications, descriptions or tests laid down in documents not forming part of the regulations.

(2) It shall be the duty of the Secretary of State, before he makes regulations under this section, to consult persons appearing to him to represent producers and users of plant and machinery with a view to ensuring that the regulations do not contain requirements which in his opinion would be impracticable or involve unreasonable expense.

(3) Any person who contravenes or causes or permits another person to contravene regulations under this section shall be guilty of an offence against this Part of this Act; but in any proceedings for a contravention of regulations made in pursuance of paragraph (*a*) of subsection (1) of this section it shall be a defence to prove that means were used for the purpose of reducing the noise in question which were not less effective for that purpose than the means required by the regulations.

(4) Without prejudice to the generality of section 104 (1) (*a*) of this Act, different regulations may be made under this section for different localities, and it shall be the duty of each local authority to enforce the provisions of regulations under this section within its area; but nothing in this section shall be taken to authorise a local authority in Scotland to institute proceedings for any offence.

(5) Nothing in this section or in regulations under this section shall be construed as derogating from any other provision of this Part of this Act. **[100]**

DEFINITIONS

Contravenes:	s. 73 (1)
Factory:	see Factories Act 1961 s. 175, as applied by subs. (1) (*b*).
Local authority:	s. 73 (1)
Noise:	s. 73 (1) and s. 73 (3)
Regulations:	made by the Secretary of State: s. 105 (1)

GENERAL NOTE

Regulations that may be made under this section relate to the level of noise caused by plant or machinery or the levels of noise caused by plant or machinery for construction works or by plant or machinery within a factory, outside the factory. Any such standards so imposed will be additional to the other requirements of Part III (see sub-s. (5)).

SUB-S. (2)

As to the duty to consult, see notes to s. 2 (3) and (4), *ante*.

Supplemental

69. Execution of works by local authority

(1) This section applies—

(*a*) to a notice under section 58 of this Act;
(*b*) to a noise reduction notice; and
(*c*) to an order of a magistrates' court under section 59 (2) or section 65 (6) of this Act,

being a notice or order which requires any person to execute any works.

(2) If that person fails to execute all or any of the works in accordance with the notice or order, the local authority may execute those works.

(3) Where a local authority execute works in pursuance of—

(*a*) section 59 (6) or section 65 (7) of this Act; or
(*b*) this section,

the local authority may recover from the person in default the expenditure incurred by the local authority in executing the works, except such of the expenditure as that person shows was unnecessary in the circumstances.

In this and the following subsection "the person in default" means—

(i) in a case under section 59 (6), the person against whom the order was made under subsection (2) of that section,
(ii) in a case under section 65 (7), the person convicted of an offence under subsection (5) of that section, and
(iii) in any other case, the person to whom the notice or order applies.

(4) In proceedings to recover any amount due to a local authority under the preceding subsection in respect of works executed by the local authority in pursuance of this section, it shall not be open to the person in default to raise any question which he could have raised on an appeal against the notice or order. **[101]**

DEFINITIONS

Local authority:	s. 73 (1)
Noise reduction notice:	s. 66 (3)
Person in default:	sub-s. (3)

GENERAL NOTE

This section, following the precedents of the Public Health and Housing Acts, gives a local authority power to execute works themselves when a person served with a notice has failed to comply. The authority will then be able to recover their necessary expenditure (*plus* establishment expenses: Local Government Act 1974, s. 36) from the person in default.

SUB-S. (1)

Section 58 and s. 59 (2) refer to nuisance abatement orders; s. 65 refers to orders made in consequence of a complaint of the registered noise level being exceeded.

SUB-S. (2)

Persons authorised by the authority will have a right of entry on the premises in order to execute the works: s. 91.

70. Appeals to Secretary of State and magistrates' court

(1) Where any provision in this Part of this Act provides for an appeal to a magistrates' court, the procedure shall be by way of complaint for an order and the Magistrates' Courts Act 1952 shall apply to the proceedings.

(2) The Secretary of State may make regulations as to appeals under this Part of this Act to the Secretary of State or, subject to the preceding subsection, to magistrates' courts; and the regulations may in particular—

(*a*) include provisions comparable to those in section 290 of the Public Health Act 1936 (appeals against notices requiring the execution of works);

(*b*) prescribe the cases in which a notice under this Part of this Act is, or is not, to be suspended until the appeal is decided, or until some other stage in the proceedings;

(*c*) prescribe the cases in which the decision on appeal may in some respects be less favourable to the appellant than the decision from which he is appealing;

(*d*) prescribe the cases in which the appellant may claim that a notice should have been served on some other person and prescribe the procedure to be followed in those cases.

(3) Regulations under this section may prescribe the procedure and practice as respect appeals to the Secretary of State under this Part of this Act, and in particular may make provision as respects—

(*a*) the particulars to be included in the notice of appeal;

(*b*) the persons on whom notice of appeal is to be served and the particulars, if any, to accompany the notice; and

(*c*) the abandonment of an appeal.

(4) In entertaining any appeal under this Part of this Act the Secretary of State, or as the case may be the magistrates' court, shall have regard to any duty imposed by law on the appellant which concerns the activities in the course of which the noise is emitted.

(5) [*Applies to Scotland only.*] [**102**]

SUB-S. (1)

As to appeals from the decisions of magistrates' courts, see s. 85 (1). The right to appeal to a magistrates' court, where one exists, must be stated in any notification of the decision of the local authority: s. 87 (5).

71. Codes of practice for minimising noise

(1) For the purpose of giving guidance on appropriate methods (including the use of specified types of plant or machinery) for minimising noise, the Secretary of State may—

(*a*) prepare and approve and issue such codes of practice as in his opinion are suitable for the purpose; and

(*b*) approve such codes of practice issued or proposed to be issued otherwise than by the Secretary of State as in the opinion of the Secretary of State are suitable for the purpose.

(2) The Secretary of State shall under paragraph (*a*) or paragraph (*b*) of the preceding subsection approve a code of practice for the carrying out of works to which section 60 of this Act applies.

(3) The powers conferred by this section on the Secretary of State shall be exercisable by order, and shall include power to vary or revoke a previous order under this section. [**103**]

DEFINITION

Noise: s. 73 (1) and s. 73 (3)

SUB-S. (1)

The power of the Secretary of State to "prepare and approve" or simply to "approve" a code of practice, must be exercised by order, made by way of statutory instrument: s. 104 (1) and sub-s. (3).

72. "Best practicable means"

(1) This section shall apply for the construction of references in this Part of this Act to best practicable means.

(2) In that expression "practicable" means reasonably practicable having regard among other things to local conditions and circumstances, to the current state of technical knowledge and to the financial implications.

(3) The means to be employed include the design, installation, maintenance and manner and periods of operation of plant and machinery, and the design, construction and maintenance of buildings and acoustic structures.

(4) The test of best practicable means is to apply only so far as compatible with any duty imposed by law, and in particular is to apply to statutory undertakers only so far as compatible with the duties imposed on them in their capacity of statutory undertakers.

(5) The said test is to apply only so far as compatible with safety and safe working conditions, and with the exigencies of any emergency or unforeseeable circumstances.

(6) Subject to the preceding provisions of this section, regard shall be had, in construing references to "best practicable means", to any relevant provision of a code of practice approved under the preceding section. **[104]**

DEFINITIONS

Code of practice:	s. 71
Statutory undertakers:	s. 73 (1)

GENERAL NOTE

The expression "best practicable means" appears in ss. 58, 59, 60 and 66. As to "reasonably practicable" (sub-s. (2)), see note to s. (3).

73. Interpretation and other supplementary provisions

(1) Except where the context otherwise requires, in this Part of this Act—

"contravention" includes a failure to comply with the provision in question, and "contravene" shall be construed accordingly;

"local authority" means—

(*a*) in England and Wales, the council of a district or a London borough, the Common Council of the City of London, the Sub-Treasurer of the Inner Temple and the Under Treasurer of the Middle Temple; and

(*b*) [*applies to Scotland only*];

"noise" includes vibration;

"noise abatement order" and "noise abatement zone" have the meanings given by section 63 of this Act;

"noise level register" has the meaning given by section 64 (2) of this Act;

"noise reduction notice" has the meaning given by section 66 (3) of this Act;

"person responsible", in relation to the emission of noise, means the person to whose act, default or sufferance the noise is attributable;

"statutory undertakers" means persons authorised by any enactment to carry on any railway, light railway, tramway, road transport, water transport, canal, inland navigation, dock, harbour, pier or lighthouse undertaking, or any undertaking for the supply of electricity, gas, hydraulic power or water, and includes the Post Office;

"work of engineering construction" means the construction, structural alteration, maintenance or repair of any railway line or siding or any dock, harbour, inland navigation, tunnel, bridge, viaduct, waterworks, reservoir, pipeline, aqueduct, sewer, sewage works or gas-holder.

(2) The area of a local authority which includes part of the seashore shall also include for the purposes of this Part of this Act, except sections 62 to 67, the territorial sea lying seawards from that part of the shore; and—

(*a*) any question as to whether a place is within the area of a local authority by virtue of this subsection shall be determined by the Secretary of State; and

(*b*) this Part of this Act (except sections 62 to 67 and this subsection) shall have effect, in relation to any area included in the area of a local authority by virtue of this subsection—

(i) as if references to premises and the occupier of premises included respectively a vessel and the master of a vessel, and

(ii) with such other modifications, if any, as are prescribed.

(3) Where more than one person is responsible for noise, this Part of this Act shall apply to each of those persons whether or not what any one of them is responsible for would by itself amount to a nuisance, or would result in a level of noise justifying action under this Part of this Act.

(4) This Part of this Act does not apply to noise caused by aircraft other than model aircraft and does not confer functions on port health authorities. **[105]**

SUB-S. (1)

As to the area of a local authority, see sub-s. (2).

SUB-S. (4)

And see Civil Aviation Act 1949, s. 40.

74. Penalties

(1) A person guilty of an offence against this Part of this Act shall be liable on summary conviction—

(*a*) in the case of a first offence against this Part of this Act, to a fine not exceeding £200; and

(*b*) in the case of a second or subsequent offence against this Part of this Act, to a fine not exceeding £400,

together, in any case, with a further fine not exceeding £50 for each day on which the offence continues after the conviction.

(2) In determining whether an offence is a second or subsequent offence against this Part of this Act, account shall be taken of any offence—

(*a*) under section 24 of the Public Health (Scotland) Act 1897 by way of contravening a decree or interdict relating to noise; or

(*b*) under section 95 of the Public Health Act 1936 by way of contravening a nuisance order relating to noise,

as if it were an offence against this Part of this Act. **[106]**

GENERAL NOTE

As to persons responsible for offences under this Part of the Act, see s. 73, sub-ss. (1) and (3).

PART IV

POLLUTION OF THE ATMOSPHERE

INTRODUCTION TO PART IV

[**107**] This is the shortest of the four substantive Parts of the Act, mainly because, as explained earlier, the principal statutes on the subject (the Alkali, etc., Works Regulation Act 1906 and the Clean Air Acts 1956 and 1968) are left virtually unrepealed.

[**108**] The most important provisions are undoubtedly ss. 75 and 76, empowering the Secretary of State to make regulations controlling the composition of motor fuel and the sulphur content of oil fuel used in central heating and other furnaces or engines (and see Introduction, p. 3, *ante*). Section 78 makes it an offence for any person to burn insulation from a cable with a view to recovering metal, unless he does so at a place registered as a "work" under the Alkali Act. Sections 79 to 83 empower local authorities (the district and London Borough Councils, the Common Council of the City, and the Temples: s. 84) to collect and publish information on atmospheric pollution in their areas, subject to the general prohibition on the disclosure of trade secrets (see s. 94, qualified in the case of general information published under s. 79 (1) (*b*)), subject to regulations made by the Secretary of State under s.82, and subject also to consultation with local industrial interests.

[**109**] It is a pity the opportunity afforded by this Act was not taken to confer the powers of the Alkali Inspectorate on the enlarged local authorities, leaving the central inspectorate to act as a research and advisory body. Indeed, the Alkali, etc., Works Regulation Act 1906, and the Regulations made thereunder are left substantially unaffected. The provisions repealed (paras. 1–4 of Sch. 3, and Sch. 4) were mainly concerned with the disposal of alkali wastes, the power of local authorities to call for the appointment of additional inspectors to serve their district (a pity this provision—s. 14—was repealed) and the power of owners of scheduled works to make special rules for the guidance of workpeople. Schedule 2, paras. 4 and 5 increases the penalties that may be imposed for offences against the 1906 Act.

Prevention of atmospheric pollution

75. Regulations about motor fuel

(1) For the purpose of limiting or reducing air pollution, the Secretary of State may by regulations—

(*a*) impose requirements as to the composition and contents of any fuel of a kind used in motor vehicles; and

(*b*) where such requirements are in force, prevent or restrict the production, treatment, distribution, import, sale or use of any fuel which in any respect fails to comply with the requirements and which is for use in the United Kingdom.

(2) It shall be the duty of the Secretary of State, before he makes any regulations in pursuance of this section, to consult such persons appearing to him to represent manufacturers and users of motor vehicles, such persons appearing to him to represent the producers and users of fuel for motor vehicles and such persons appearing to him to be conversant with problems of air pollution as he considers appropriate.

(3) Regulations under this section—

(*a*) in imposing requirements as to the composition and contents of any fuel, may apply standards, specifications, descriptions or tests laid down in documents not forming part of the regulations;

(*b*) may authorise the Secretary of State to confer exemptions from any provision of the regulations.

(4) Where fuel is subject to requirements as to composition or contents imposed by regulations under this section, the regulations may, in order that persons to whom the fuel is supplied are afforded information as to its composition or contents, impose requirements for securing that the information is displayed at such places and in such manner as may be prescribed by the regulations.

(5) It shall be the duty of every local weights and measures authority to enforce the provisions of regulations under this section within its area; and subsections (2) and (3) of section 26 of the Trade Descriptions Act 1968 (reports and inquiries) shall apply as respects those authorities' functions under this subsection as they apply to their functions under that Act.

(6) The following provisions of the Trade Descriptions Act 1968 shall apply in relation to the enforcement of regulations under this section as they apply to the enforcement of that Act, that is to say—

section 27 (power to make test purchases);
section 28 (power to enter premises and inspect and seize goods and documents);
section 29 (obstruction of authorised officers);
section 30 (notice of test),

and section 33 of that Act shall apply to the exercise of powers under section 28 as applied by this subsection.

References to an offence under that Act in those provisions as applied by this subsection, except the reference in section 30 (2) to an offence under section 28 (5) or 29 of that Act, shall be construed as references to an offence under section 77 of this Act relating to regulations under this section.

(7) [*Applies to Scotland only.*]

(8) and (9) [Applies to Northern Ireland only.] [**110**]

DEFINITIONS

Local weights and measures authority:	the county councils and London borough councils in England, and the county councils and designated district councils in Wales: Local Government Act 1972, s. 201
Regulations:	made by the Secretary of State: s. 105 (1)

GENERAL NOTE

Regulations may be made under this section imposing requirements as to the composition and contents of motor vehicle fuel, but only for the purpose of limiting or reducing air pollution. The regulations may apply only to fuel and not to oil as used as a lubricant. As to offences against the regulations, see s. 77.

SUB-S. (1)

See also the powers given by s. 100 to prohibit or restrict the importation and use of specified injurious substances.

SUB-S. (2)

As to consultation, see note on s. 2 (3).

76. Regulations about sulphur content of oil fuel for furnaces or engines

(1) For the purpose of limiting or reducing air pollution, the Secretary of State may by regulations impose limits on the sulphur content of oil fuel which is used in furnaces or engines.

(2) It shall be the duty of the Secretary of State, before he makes any regulations in pursuance of this section, to consult such persons appearing to him to represent producers and users of oil fuel, such persons appearing to him to represent manufacturers and users of plant and equipment for which oil fuel is used and such persons appearing to him to be conversant with problems of air pollution as he considers appropriate.

(3) Regulations under this section—

(*a*) may prescribe the kinds of oil fuel, and the kinds of furnaces and engines, to which the regulations are to apply;

(*b*) may apply standards, specifications, descriptions or tests laid down in documents not forming part of the regulations;

(*c*) may authorise the Secretary of State to confer exemptions from any provision of the regulations;

(*d*) may, without prejudice to the generality of section 104 (1) (*a*) of this Act, make different provision for different areas.

(4) It shall be the duty—

(*a*) of every local authority to enforce the provisions of regulations under this section within its area, except in relation to a furnace which is part of a work subject to the Alkali Act; and

(*b*) of the inspectors appointed under that Act to enforce those provisions in relation to such furnaces;

but nothing in this section shall be taken to authorise a local authority in Scotland to institute proceedings for any offence.

(5) In this section "oil fuel" means any liquid petroleum product produced in a refinery. [**111**]

DEFINITIONS

Alkali Act:	s. 105 (1)
Local authority:	s. 84 (1)
Oil fuel:	sub-s. (5)
Regulations:	made by the Secretary of State: s. 105 (1)
Work subject to the Alkali Act:	s. 84 (1)

GENERAL NOTE

This section supplements s. 75, in that regulations made hereunder may limit the sulphur content of oil fuel used for central heating and other furnaces and for engines (whether in vehicles or fixed at premises); but again only for the purpose of limiting or reducing air pollution. Regulations under this section, will be enforceable by local authorities and not (as is the case with s. 75) by weights and measures authorities, except in so far as enforcement will be the responsibility of the Alkali Inspectorate. As to offences against the regulations, see s. 77.

SUB-S. (2)

As to consultation, see note on s. 2 (3)

SUB-S. (5)

This definition seems to bring within the meaning of the expression any such product, whether or not used as "fuel".

77. Provisions supplementary to ss. 75 and 76

(1) A person who contravenes or fails to comply with any provision of regulations under either of the two preceding sections shall be guilty of an offence and liable—

(*a*) on conviction on indictment to a fine; and
(*b*) on summary conviction to a fine not exceeding £400:

Provided that the regulations may in any case exclude liability to conviction on indictment, and may in any case reduce the maximum fine on summary conviction.

(2) Regulations under each of the two preceding sections shall, subject to any provision to the contrary in the regulations, apply to fuel used for, and to persons in, the public service of the Crown as they apply to fuel used for other purposes and to other persons; but a local authority shall not be entitled by virtue of this subsection to exercise, in relation to fuel used for and persons in that service, any power conferred on the authority by virtue of sections 91 to 93 of this Act. [**112**]

DEFINITIONS

Local authority:	s. 84 (1)
Regulations:	made by the Secretary of State: s. 105 (1)

78. Cable burning

(1) A person who burns insulation from a cable with a view to recovering metal from the cable shall be guilty of an offence under this subsection unless the place at which he does so is a work registered in pursuance of section 9 of the Alkali Act.

(2) Section 16A of the Alkali Act (which, as amended by this Act, provides that certain offences under that Act shall be punishable on summary conviction by a fine not exceeding £400 or £50 a day in the case of certain continuing offences and that proceedings for the offences shall not be brought in England and Wales except by an inspector or with the consent of the Secretary of State) shall apply to an offence under the preceding subsection as it applies to the offences mentioned in that section. [**113**]

DEFINITION

Alkali Act:	see s. 105 (1)

Information about atmospheric pollution

79. Research and publicity

(1) A local authority may—

(*a*) undertake, or contribute towards the cost of, investigation and research relevant to the problem of air pollution; and
(*b*) arrange for the publication of information on that problem.

(2) Without prejudice to the generality of the preceding subsection, local authorities may obtain information about the emission of pollutants and other substances into the air—

(*a*) by issuing notices under the following section; and
(*b*) by measuring and recording the omissions, and for that purpose

entering on any premises, whether by agreement or in exercise of the power conferred by section 91 of this Act; and

(*c*) by entering into arrangements with occupiers of premises under which they measure and record emissions on behalf of the local authority;

but references to premises in paragraphs (*b*) and (*c*) of this subsection do not include private dwellings.

(3) A local authority shall not be entitled to exercise the power mentioned in paragraph (*b*) of the preceding subsection for the purpose of measuring and recording such emissions on any premises unless—

(*a*) the authority has given to the occupier of the premises a notice—

(i) specifying the kind of emissions in question and the steps it proposes to take on the premises for the purpose of measuring and recording emissions of that kind, and

(ii) stating that it proposes to exercise that power for that purpose unless the occupier makes a request to the authority in pursuance of the following provisions of this subsection; and

(*b*) the period of twenty-one days beginning with the day on which the notice was given has expired,

and shall not be entitled to exercise that power in consequence of the notice if during that period the occupier gives a notice to the authority requesting it to serve on him a notice under the following section with respect to the emissions.

(4) Nothing in this section shall authorise a local authority to investigate emissions from any work subject to the Alkali Act otherwise than by issuing notices under the following section, or by exercising the powers conferred on the authority by subsection (1) (*a*) of this section without entering the work.

(5) In acting under subsection (1) (*b*) of this section, a local authority shall ensure that the material published is presented in such a way that no information relating to a trade secret is disclosed except with the consent in writing of a person authorised to disclose it or with the consent of the Secretary of State.

(6) Breach of a duty imposed by the preceding subsection shall be actionable; but in any proceedings, whether civil or criminal, brought against a local authority, or any member or officer of a local authority, on the grounds that any information has been published, it shall be a defence to show that it was published in compliance with the preceding provisions of this section.

(7) The preceding subsection applies in particular to any proceedings brought under section 26 of the Clean Air Act 1956 (which, as amended by subsection (10) of this section, makes it an offence to disclose information relating to any trade secret).

(8) So long as a local authority exercises any of its powers under subsection (2) of this section, it shall from time to time consult such persons carrying on any trade or business in the authority's area, or such organisations appearing to the authority to be representative of those persons, and such persons appearing to the authority to be conversant with problems of air pollution or to have an interest in local amenity as appear to the authority to be appropriate—

(*a*) about the way in which the local authority exercises its powers under this and the following section; and

(*b*) about the extent to which, and the manner in which, any information collected under those powers should be made available to the public.

(9) The consultations shall take place from time to time as the authority think necessary, but not less than twice in each financial year.

(10) Paragraphs (*a*) and (*b*) of section 25 of the Clean Air Act 1956 (which are superseded by the provisions of this section) shall cease to have effect, and in paragraph (*c*) of that section for the words "that problem" there shall be substituted the words "the problem of the pollution of the air"; and in section 26 of that Act (which relates to the unjustified disclosure of information relating to any manufacturing process or trade secret) the words "manufacturing process or" shall cease to have effect. [**114**]

DEFINITIONS

Emission:	s. 84 (2)
Local authority:	s. 84 (1)
Premises:	s. 105 (1)
Private dwelling:	s. 84 (1) and s. 30 (1)
Work subject to the Alkali Act:	s. 84 (1)

GENERAL NOTE

This elaborately detailed section, supplemented by ss. 80–82, empowers a local authority to engage in investigation and research into air pollution and to publish information (but not in breach of a trade secret) on the subject. They may also measure emissions and take samples (subs. (2) but see subs. (3)). "Measurement" includes a power to take samples: s. 84 (3). These functions must be performed in accordance with regulations made under s. 82, but this section and s. 74 empower the authority to serve notices on the occupiers of premises (other than private dwellings) requiring the furnishing of information about air pollution. As to Crown premises, see s. 80 (6).

SUB-S. (1)

Publication of information; but see sub-s. (5).

SUB-S. (2)

But an authority may not concern themselves (otherwise than by issuing notices or using their powers under sub-s. (1) (*a*)) with emissions from premises registered under the Alkali, etc. Works Regulation Act 1906: sub-s. (4). See also the preliminary procedure required under sub-s. (3). Information obtained under this subsection may have to be recorded in a register maintained under regulations made under s. 82 (2).

SUB-S. (3)

Such a notice should be served in accordance with s. 233 of the Local Government Act 1972.

SUB-S. (8)

As to consultations, see note to s. 2 (2), and sub-s. (9).

SUB-S. (10)

The provisions of s. 25 of the 1956 Act refer to the powers of local authorities as to research and publicity.

80. Notices requiring information about air pollution

(1) A local authority may by notice require the occupier of any premises in its area to furnish, whether by periodical returns or by other means, such estimates or other information as may be specified or described in the notice concerning the emission of pollutants and other substances into the air from the premises.

(2) This section shall not apply to premises in so far as they consist of a private dwelling.

(3) If the notice relates to a work subject to the Alkali Act, the person on whom the notice is served shall not be obliged to supply any information which, as certified by an inspector appointed under that Act, is not of a kind which is being supplied to the inspector for the purposes of that Act.

(4) The person on whom a notice is served under this section shall comply with the notice within six weeks of the date of service or within such longer period as the local authority may by notice allow.

(5) A notice under this section shall not require returns at intervals of less than three months, and no one notice (whether or not requiring periodical returns shall call for information covering a period of more than twelve months.

(6) Except so far as regulations provide otherwise, this section shall apply to premises used for, and to persons in, the public service of the Crown as it applies to other premises and persons; but a local authority shall not be entitled by virtue of this subsection to exercise, in relation to premises used for and persons in that service, any power conferred on the authority by virtue of sections 91 to 93 of this Act.

(7) A person who—

(*a*) fails without reasonable excuse to comply with the requirements of a notice served on him in pursuance of this section; or

(*b*) in furnishing any estimate or other information in compliance with a notice under this section, makes any statement which he knows to be false in a material particular or recklessly makes any statement which is false in a material particular,

shall be guilty of an offence and liable on summary conviction to a fine not exceeding £400.

(8) Where a person is convicted of an offence under the preceding subsection in respect of any premises and information of any kind, nothing in subsection (3) of the preceding section shall prevent a local authority from exercising the power of entry there mentioned for the purpose of obtaining information of that kind in respect of the premises. **[115]**

DEFINITIONS

Emission:	s. 84 (2)
Local authority:	s. 84 (1)
Premises:	s. 105 (1)
Private dwelling:	s. 84 (1) and s. 30 (1)
Regulations:	made by the Secretary of State: s. 105 (1)
Work subject to the Alkali Act:	s. 84 (1)

GENERAL NOTE

This section is purely procedural, dealing with notices to be served by a local authority for the purpose of performing their functions under s. 79. Appeals lie against these notices under s. 81. Compare the powers given by s. 93.

SUB-S. (1)

Such notices should be served in accordance with s. 233 of the Local Government Act 1972. "Any premises": but not a private dwelling: sub-s. (2).

SUB-S. (4)

As to failure to comply, see sub-s. (7).

81. Appeals against notices

(1) A person served with a notice under the preceding section, or any other person having an interest in the premises to which the notice relates, may appeal to the Secretary of State—

(*a*) on the ground that the giving to the authority or the disclosure to the public of all or part of the information required by the notice would—

(i) prejudice to an unreasonable degree some private interest by disclosing information about a trade secret, or

(ii) be contrary to the public interest, or

(*b*) on the ground that the information required by the notice is not immediately available and cannot readily be collected or obtained by the recipient of the notice without incurring undue expenditure for the purpose.

(2) If the Secretary of State allows the appeal he may direct the local authority to withdraw or modify the notice, or to take such steps as may be specified by the Secretary of State to ensure that prejudicial information is not disclosed to the public; and it shall be the duty of the authority to comply with the direction.

(3) The Secretary of State may make regulations as to appeals under this section, including regulations about the time for bringing an appeal and the circumstances in which all or any part of the appellant's case is to be withheld from the respondent; but it shall be the duty of the Secretary of State, before he makes any regulations under this subsection, to consult such persons appearing to him to represent local authorities, such persons appearing to him to represent industrial interests and such persons appearing to him to be conversant with problems of air pollution as he considers appropriate. [**116**]

DEFINITIONS

Local authority:	s. 84 (1)
Premises:	s. 105 (1)
Regulations:	s. 105 (1)

GENERAL NOTE

Note the restricted ground on which an appeal against a notice served under s. 80 may be based. Procedure on such appeals may be specified in regulations (sub-s. (3)), and because of the possibility of secrets being involved, the regulations may provide that part of the appellant's case shall be withheld from the respondent local authority.

SUB-S. (3)

As to consultation, see note to s. 2 (3).

82. Regulations about research and publicity

(1) The Secretary of State shall by regulations prescribe the manner in which, and the methods by which, local authorities are to perform their functions under sections 79 and 80 of this Act.

(2) It shall be the duty of the Secretary of State, before he makes regulations under this section, to consult such persons appearing to him to represent local authorities, such persons appearing to him to represent industrial interests and such persons appearing to him to be conversant with problems of air pollution as he considers appropriate.

(3) Regulations under this section may in particular—

(*a*) prescribe the kinds of emissions to which notices under section 80 of this Act may relate;

(*b*) prescribe the kinds of information which may be required by those notices;

(*c*) prescribe the manner in which any such notice is to be given, and the evidence which is to be sufficient evidence of its having been given, and of its contents and authenticity;

(*d*) require each local authority to maintain in a prescribed form a register containing—

(i) information obtained by the authority by virtue of section 79 (2) of this Act, other than information as to which a direction in pursuance of subsection (2) of the preceding section provides that the information is not to be disclosed to the public; and

(ii) such information (if any) as the Secretary of State may determine, or as may be determined by or under regulations, with respect to any appeal in pursuance of the preceding section which was against a notice served by the authority and which the Secretary of State did not dismiss;

(*e*) specify the circumstances in which local authorities may enter into arrangements with owners or occupiers of premises under which they will record and measure emissions on behalf of the local authorities;

(*f*) specify the kinds of apparatus which local authorities are to have power to provide and use for measuring and recording emissions and for other purposes.

(4) Regulations under subsection (3) (*b*) of this section may in particular require returns of—

(*a*) the total volume of gases, whether pollutant or not, discharged from the premises in question over any period;

(*b*) the concentration of pollutant in the gases discharged;

(*c*) the total of the pollutant discharged over any period;

(*d*) the height or heights at which discharges take place;

(*e*) the hours during which discharges take place;

(*f*) the concentration of pollutants at ground level.

(5) A register maintained by a local authority in pursuance of regulations made by virtue of subsection (3) (*d*) of this section shall be open to public inspection at the principal office of the authority free of charge at all reasonable hours, and the authority shall afford members of the public reasonable facilities for obtaining from the authority, on payment of reasonable charges, copies of entries in the register. **[117]**

DEFINITIONS

Emission	s. 84 (2)
Local authority:	s. 84 (1)
Premises:	s. 105 (1)
Regulations:	s. 105 (1)

SUB-S. (2)

Consultation: see note to s. 2 (3)).

SUB-S. (3)

The register has to be open to public inspection: sub-s. (5).

83. Provision by local authorities of information for Secretary of State

(1) The Secretary of State may, for the purpose of obtaining information about air pollution, direct a local authority to make such arrangements as may be specified in the direction—

(*a*) for the provision, installation, operation and maintenance by the local authority of apparatus for measuring and recording air pollution; and

(*b*) for transmitting the information so obtained to the Secretary of State.

(2) Where apparatus is provided in pursuance of a direction under the preceding subsection, the Secretary of State shall defray the whole of the capital expenditure incurred by a local authority in providing and installing the apparatus.

(3) Before giving a direction under subsection (1) of this section the Secretary of State shall consult the local authority, and it shall be the duty of the local authority to comply with any direction given under that subsection. **[118]**

DEFINITION

Local authority: s. 84 (1)

SUB-S. (1)

Such a direction need not be made by way of statutory instrument. "Measurement" includes taking samples: s. 84 (3).

SUB-S. (3)

Consultation: see note to s. 2 (3).

Interpretation

84. Interpretation of Part IV

(1) In this Part of this Act—

"local authority" means—

(*a*) in England and Wales, the council of a district or a London borough, the Common Council of the City of London, the Sub-Treasurer of the Inner Temple and the Under Treasurer of the Middle Temple, and

(*b*) [*applies to Scotland only.*];

"private dwelling" has the same meaning as in Part I of this Act; and

"a work subject to the Alkali Act" means a work registered under section 9 of the Alkali Act, excluding the whole or part of such a work while the work or part is the subject of an order made or treated as made under subsection (3) of section 11 of the Clean Air Act 1968 (under which certain enactments relating to clean air which apart from that subsection do not apply to works so registered may be applied to such works).

(2) References in this Part of this Act to the emission of substances into the atmosphere shall be construed as applying to substances in a gaseous or liquid or solid state, or any combination of those states.

(3) Any reference in this Part of this Act to measurement includes a reference to the taking of samples. **[119]**

DEFINITIONS

Alkali Act: s. 105 (1)

Premises: s. 105 (1)

PART V
SUPPLEMENTARY PROVISIONS

Legal proceedings

85. Appeals to Crown Court or Court of Session against decisions of magistrates' court or sheriff

(1) An appeal against any decision of a magistrates' court in pursuance of this Act (other than a decision made in criminal proceedings) shall lie to the Crown Court at the instance of any party to the proceedings in which the decision was given if such an appeal does not lie to the Crown Court by virtue of any other enactment.

(2) [*Applies to Scotland only.*]

(3) Where a person appeals to the Crown Court or the Court of Session against a decision of a magistrates' court or the sheriff dismissing an appeal against a notice served in pursuance of this Act which was suspended pending determination of that appeal, the notice shall again be suspended pending the determination of the appeal to the Crown Court or Court of Session. [**120**]

GENERAL NOTE

This is by way of "tidying up" section, in that it ensures there shall be a right of appeal to the Crown Court from a decision of magistrates, either on appeal to them, or on a complaint (for example, under s. 59).

86. Protection of members and officers of authorities from personal liability

(1) Section 265 of the Public Health Act 1875 (which relates to the protection from personal liability of members and officers of certain authorities when acting under the direction of the authorities) shall have effect as if references to those authorities and that Act included respectively references to water authorities and this Act.

(2) This section does not apply to Scotland. [**121**]

GENERAL NOTE

This is a common form section to be found in administrative statutes of this kind.

87. Miscellaneous provisions relating to legal proceedings

(1) When an offence under this Act which has been committed by a body corporate is proved to have been committed with the consent or connivance of, or to be attributable to any neglect on the part of, any director, manager, secretary or other similar officer of the body corporate or any person who was purporting to act in any such capacity, he as well as the body corporate shall be guilty of that offence and be liable to be proceeded against and punished accordingly.

Where the affairs of a body corporate are managed by its members the preceding provisions of this subsection shall apply in relation to the acts and defaults of a member in connection with his functions of management as if he were a director of the body corporate.

(2) Where the commission by any person of an offence under this Act is due to the act or default of some other person, that other person shall be guilty of

the offence; and a person may be charged with and convicted of an offence by virtue of this subsection whether or not proceedings for the offence are taken against any other person.

(3) Notwithstanding anything in section 104 of the Magistrates' Courts Act 1952, a magistrates' court in England and Wales may try an information for an offence under section 3 (2) or (3) of this Act or by virtue of section 18 (2) of this Act or under section 31 (1) of this Act or regulations or byelaws made in pursuance of section 31 of this Act if the information is laid within one year from the commission of the offence; . . .

(4) Where an appeal against a decision of a relevant authority lies to a magistrates' court by virtue of any provision of this Act, it shall be the duty of the authority to include in any document by which it notifies the decision to the person concerned a statement indicating that such an appeal lies as aforesaid and specifying the time within which it must be brought.

(5) Where on an appeal to any court against or arising out of a decision of a relevant authority in pursuance of this Act the court varies or reverses the decision it shall be the duty of the authority to act in accordance with the court's decision.

(6) A judge of any court and a justice of the peace shall not be disqualified from acting in cases arising under this Act by reason of his being, as one of several ratepayers or as one of any other class of persons, liable in common with the others to contribute to or be benefited by any rate or fund out of which any expenses of a relevant authority are to be defrayed. [**122**]

DEFINITION

Relevant authority: s. 98

SUB-S. (1)

As to offences by corporations, see *Tesco Supermarkets, Ltd.* v. *Nattrass*, [1972] A.C. 153; [1971] 2 All E.R. 127.

SUB-S. (3)

The usual time limit for summary proceedings under s. 104 is six months.

88. Civil liability for contravention of s. 3 (3)

(1) Where any damage is caused by poisonous, noxious or polluting waste which has been deposited on land, any person who deposited it or caused or knowingly permitted it to be deposited, in either case so as to commit an offence under section 3 (3) or by virtue of section 18 (2) of this Act, is liable for the damage except where the damage—

(*a*) was due wholly to the fault of the person who suffered it; or

(*b*) was suffered by a person who voluntarily accepted the risk thereof.

(2) The matters which under paragraphs (*a*) to (*c*) of subsection (4) of section 3 of this Act may be proved by way of defence to a charge of committing an offence under subsection (3) of that section may be proved also by way of defence to an action brought by virtue of the preceding subsection (the reference in the said paragraph (*a*) to the charge being construed as a reference to the act alleged to give rise to the liability).

(3) In this section—

"damage" includes the death of, or injury to, any person (including any disease and any impairment of physical or mental condition);

"fault" has the same meaning as in the Law Reform (Contributory Negligence) Act 1945; and

"land" includes such water as is mentioned in section 4 (4) of this Act.

(4) For the purposes of the following enactments, namely—

(*a*) the Fatal Accidents Acts 1846 to 1959;

(*b*) the Law Reform (Contributory Negligence) Act 1945; and

(*c*) the Limitation Acts 1939 and 1963 and the Law Reform (Limitation of Actions, &c.) Act 1954,

and for the purposes of any action of damages in Scotland arising out of the death of, or personal injury to, any person, any damage for which a person is liable under subsection (1) of this section shall be treated as due to his fault.

(5) Subsection (1) of this section is without prejudice to any liability which arises apart from the provisions of this section. [**123**]

DEFINITIONS

Damage:	sub-s. (3)
Fault:	sub-s. (3)
Land:	sub-s. (3) and s. 4 (4)
Waste:	see s. 30 (1), which applies only for the purposes of Part I.

SUB-S. (1)

As to actions arising out of death or personal injury, see sub-s. (4).

Financial provisions

89. Expenses and receipts of Secretary of State, etc.

(1) There shall be paid out of money provided by Parliament—

(*a*) any expenses incurred by the Secretary of State for the purposes of this Act; and

(*b*) any increase attributable to the provisions of this Act in the sums payable under any other Act out of money so provided.

(2) Any sums received by the Secretary of State by virtue of this Act shall be paid into the Consolidated Fund. [**124**]

90. Establishment charges and interest in respect of certain expenses of authorities

(1) Where a sum is payable to a water authority by any person by virtue of this Act in respect of the expenses incurred by the authority, the authority shall be entitled to recover from that person such a further sum in respect of its establishment charges as appears to the authority to be reasonable.

(2) Where such a sum or further sum as is mentioned in the preceding subsection is payable to a water authority by any person or a sum is payable to any other relevant authority by any person by virtue of this Act in respect of the expenses incurred by the authority or by virtue of section 36 of the Local Government Act 1974 in respect of establishment charges related to such expenses or by virtue of section 193 of the Local Government (Scotland) Act 1947 in respect of general expenses related to such expenses, then—

(*a*) the authority and that person may agree that the sum or further sum shall be paid in instalments; and

(*b*) the authority shall be entitled to receive from that person interest on the sum or further sum, or on such portion of it as is for the time being unpaid, at the rate fixed by subsection (2) of section 171 of the Local Government Act 1972 or, in Scotland, subsection (2) of section 121 of the Local Government (Scotland) Act 1973 (which fix a rate of one quarter per cent. above the rate determined by the Treasury in relation to the loans mentioned in that subsection).

(3) [*Applies to Scotland only.*] **[125]**

DEFINITIONS

Relevant authority:	s. 98
Water authority:	Water Act 1973, s. 2

SUB-S. (1)

Compare s. 36 of the Local Government Act 1973.

SUB-S. (2)

The rate of interest is fixed at one quarter per cent above the relevant rate determined by the Treasury in relation to local loans under the National Loans Act 1968.

Miscellaneous

91. Rights of entry and inspection, etc.

(1) Any person authorised in writing in that behalf by a relevant authority may at any reasonable time—

(*a*) enter upon any land or vessel for the purpose of—

(i) performing any function conferred on the authority or that person by virtue of this Act, or

(ii) determining whether, and if so in what manner, such a function should be performed, or

(iii) determing whether any provision of this Act or of an instrument made by virtue of this Act is being complied with;

(*b*) carry out such inspections, measurements and tests on the land or vessel or of any articles on it and take away such samples of the land or articles as he considers appropriate for such a purpose.

(2) If it is shown to the satisfaction of a justice of the peace on sworn information in writing—

(*a*) that admission to any land or vessel which a person is entitled to enter in pursuance of the preceding sub-section has been refused to that person or that refusal is apprehended or that the land or vessel is unoccupied or that the occupier is temporarily absent or that the case is one of emergency or that an application for admission would defeat the object of the entry; and

(*b*) that there is reasonable ground for entry upon the land or vessel for the purpose for which entry is required,

then, subject to the following subsection, the justice may by warrant under his hand authorise that person to enter the land or vessel, if need be by force.

(3) A justice of the peace shall not issue a warrant in pursuance of the preceding subsection in respect of any land or vessel unless he is satisfied—

(*a*) that admission to the land or vessel in pursuance of subsection (1) of this section was sought after not less than seven days notice of the intended entry had been served on the occupier; or

(*b*) that admission to the land or vessel in pursuance of that subsection was sought in an emergency and was refused by or on behalf of the occupier; or

(*c*) that the land or vessel is unoccupied; or

(*d*) that an application for admission to the land or vessel would defeat the object of the entry.

(4) A warrant issued in pursuance of this section shall continue in force until the purpose for which the entry is required has been satisfied.

(5) [*Applies to Scotland only.*] [**126**]

DEFINITIONS

Functions:	s. 98
Relevant authority:	s. 98
Vessel:	s. 105 (1)

GENERAL NOTE

This section should be read as one with s. 92. The section confers a wide power of entry on land on local and water authorities to enable them to carry out their powers and duties under the Act, but it does not, in particular, extend to their power to collect information about, or to make arrangements for the disposal of waste (other than controlled waste) under s. 19.

SUB-S. (1)

As to the authentication of the status of an "authorised person", see s. 234 of the Local Government Act 1972 and para. 19 of Sch. 3 to the Water Act 1973. "Instrument" is not defined for the purpose of this Act, but it presumably includes regulations and orders and also notices and directions given in writing.

SUB-S. (3)

Service of this notice should be effected in accordance either (as the case may be) with s. 233 of the Local Government Act 1972, or with s. 95 of this Act. As to "emergency", see s. 92 (7).

92. Provisions supplementary to s. 91

(1) A person authorised to enter upon any land or vessel in pursuance of the preceding section shall, if so required, produce evidence of his authority before he enters upon the land or vessel.

(2) A person so authorised may take with him on to the land or vessel in question such other persons and such equipment as may be necessary.

(3) Admission to any land or vessel used for residential purposes and admission with heavy equipment to any other land or vessel shall not, except in an emergency or in a case where the land or vessel is unoccupied, be demanded as of right in pursuance of subsection (1) of the preceding section unless a notice of the intended entry has been served on the occupier not less than seven days before the demand.

(4) A person who, in the exercise of powers conferred on him by virtue of the preceding section or this section, enters upon any land or vessel which is unoccupied or of which the occupier is temporarily absent shall leave the land or vessel as effectually secured against trespassers as he found it.

(5) It shall be the duty of a relevant authority to make full compensation to any person who has sustained damage by reason of—

(*a*) the exercise by a person authorised by the authority of any powers conferred on the person so authorised by virtue of the preceding section or this section; or

(*b*) the failure of a person so authorised to perform the duty imposed on him by the preceding subsection,

except where the damage is attributable to the default of the person who sustained it; and any dispute as to a person's entitlement to compensation in pursuance of this subsection or as to the amount of the compensation shall be determined by arbitration.

(6) A person who wilfully obstructs another person acting in the exercise of any powers conferred on the other person by virtue of the preceding section or this section shall be guilty of an offence and liable on summary conviction to a fine not exceeding £100.

(7) In the preceding section and this section any reference to an emergency is a reference to a case where a person requiring entry to any land or vessel has reasonable cause to believe that circumstances exist which are likely to endanger life or health and that immediate entry to the land or vessel is necessary to verify the existence of those circumstances or to ascertain their cause or to effect a remedy. [**127**]

DEFINITION

Vessel: s. 105 (1)

SUB-S. (1)

See note to s. 91 (1).

SUB-S. (3)

As to "emergency", see sub-s. (7). Service of such a notice should be effected in accordance with s. 233 of the Local Government Act 1972 or s. 95 of this Act, as the case may be.

SUB-S. (5)

Any arbitration under this subsection will be subject to the Arbitration Act 1950: see s. 31 (1) thereof.

SUB-S. (6)

"Wilfully obstructs": see *Hinchcliffe* v. *Sheldon*, [1955] 3 All E.R. 406, and the earlier case of *Betts* v. *Stevens*, [1910] 1 K.B.1.

93. Power of authorities to obtain information

(1) Subject to the following subsection, a relevant authority may serve on any person a notice requiring him to furnish to the authority, within a period or at times specified in the notice and in a form so specified, any information so specified which the authority reasonably considers that it needs for the purposes of any function conferred on the authority by this Act.

(2) Provision may be made by regulations for restricting the information which may be required in pursuance of the preceding subsection and for determining the form in which the information is to be so required.

(3) A person who—

(*a*) fails without reasonable excuse to comply with the requirements of a notice served on him in pursuance of this section; or

(*b*) in furnishing any information in compliance with such a notice, makes any statement which he knows to be false in a material particular or recklessly makes any statement which is false in a material particular,

shall be guilty of an offence and liable on summary conviction to a fine not exceeding £400.

(4) [*Applies to Scotland only.*] [**128**]

DEFINITIONS

Functions:	s. 98
Regulations:	made by the Secretary of State: s. 105 (1)
Relevant authority:	s. 98

GENERAL NOTE

This section should be read with other powers relating to this topic. These are s. 19 (collecting of information as to waste other than controlled waste), s. 50 (closure of mines), and ss. 79–83 (information as to air pollution). See also s. 25 of the Clean Air Act 1956 (as amended). The section will be of particular value when (for example) a disposal authority is preparing its plan under s. 2.

SUB-S. (1)

Service of such a notice should be effected in accordance with s. 233 of the Local Government Act 1972, or s. 89 of this Act, as the case may be.

94. Prohibition of disclosure of information

(1) If a person discloses information relating to any trade secret used in carrying on a particular undertaking and the information has been given to him or obtained by him by virtue of this Act he shall, subject to the following subsection, be guilty of an offence and liable on summary conviction to a fine not exceeding £400.

(2) A person shall not be guilty of an offence under the preceding subsection by virtue of the disclosure of any information if—

(*a*) the disclosure is made—

(i) in the performance of his duty, or

(ii) in pursuance of section 79 (1) (*b*) of this Act, or

(iii) with the consent in writing of a person having a right to disclose the information; or

(*b*) the information is of a kind prescribed for the purposes of this paragraph and, if regulations made for those purposes provide that information of that kind may only be disclosed in pursuance of the regulations to prescribed persons, the disclosure is to a prescribed person.

(3) [*Applies to Scotland only.*] [**129**]

DEFINITIONS

Prescribed:	by regulations: s. 105 (1)
Regulations:	made by the Secretary of State: s. 105 (1)

GENERAL NOTE

As to the disclosure of trade secrets, see the Introduction to the Act p. 4, *ante*.

95. Service of documents on and by water authorities

(1) Any document required or authorised by virtue of this Act to be served on a water authority shall be so served by addressing it to the authority and leaving it at or sending it by post to the principal office of the authority or any other office specified by the authority as one at which it will accept documents of the same kind as that document.

(2) Any document required or authorised by virtue of this Act to be served on a person by a water authority may be so served—

(*a*) by delivering it to him or by leaving it at his proper address or by sending it by post to him at that address; or

(*b*) if the person is a body corporate, by serving it in accordance with the preceding paragraph on the secretary or clerk of that body; or

(*c*) if the person is a partnership, by serving it as aforesaid on a partner or a person having the control or management of the partnership business.

(3) For the purposes of this section and section 26 of the Interpretation Act 1889 (which relates to the service of documents by post) in its application to this section, the proper address of any person on whom a document is to be served by a water authority shall be his last known address, except that—

(*a*) in the case of service on a body corporate or its secretary or clerk it shall be the address of the registered or principal office of the body;

(*b*) in the case of service on a partnership or a partner or a person having the control or management of the partnership business it shall be the principal office of the partnership;

and for the purposes of this subsection the principal office of a company registered outside the United Kingdom or of a partnership carrying on business outside the United Kingdom is its principal office within the United Kingdom.

(4) If a person to be served by virtue of this Act with any document by a water authority has specified an address within the United Kingdom other than his proper address (as determined in pursuance of the preceding subsection) as the one at which he or someone on his behalf will accept documents of the same kind as that document, that address shall also be treated as his proper address for the purposes of this section and the said section 26 in its application to this section.

(5) If the name or address of any owner or occupier of land on whom by virtue of this Act any document is to be served by a water authority cannot after reasonable inquiry be ascertained, the document may be served either by leaving it in the hands of a person who is or appears to be resident or employed on the land or by leaving it conspicuously affixed to some building or object on the land.

(6) Nothing in the preceding provisions of this section relates to service of a document in proceedings in court.

(7) This section shall not apply to Scotland. [**130**]

DEFINITION

Water authority: Water Act 1973, s. 2

GENERAL NOTE

This section was brought into force on 12th December 1974 by The Control of Pollution Act 1974 (Commencement No. 1) Order 1974 (S.I. 1974 No. 2039). applies only to water authorities; the service of notices on and by local authorities is provided for by ss. 231 and 233 of the Local Government Act 1972, which it closely resembles. There is no specific power to serve a notice requiring information as to ownership, on the occupier of any premises (cf. s. 233 (6) of the 1972 Act), but as most notices under this Act are required to be served on a "person" or the "person responsible" (Part III), or sometimes on "the occupier", information as to the owner of premises will be rarely required. Where it is so required, presumably a notice could be served under s. 93 (1), subject to any regulations made under s. 93 (2).

96. Local inquiries

(1) The Secretary of State may cause a local inquiry to be held in any case in which he considers it appropriate for such an inquiry to be held either in connection with a provision of this Act or with a view to preventing or dealing with pollution or noise at any place.

(2) Subsections (2) to (5) of section 250 of the Local Government Act 1972 (which contain supplementary provisions with respect to local inquiries held in pursuance of that section) shall, without prejudice to the generality of subsection (1) of that section, apply to inquiries in England and Wales in pursuance of the preceding subsection as they apply to inquiries in pursuance of that section but as if the reference to a local authority in subsection (4) included a reference to a water authority.

(3) [*Applies to Scotland only.*] **[131]**

SUB-S. (1)

"Pollution" here is presumably to be understood as referring to pollution by waste on land, the pollution of water, or atmospheric pollution. In other words, the powers of the Secretry of State should be read within the confines of the present Act. "Noise" presumably includes vibration: see s. 73 (1).

SUB-S. (2)

These provisions of s. 250 are concerned with the issue of a summons requiring an individual to attend and give evidence at the inquiry, and also with the question of costs.

97. Default powers

(1) If the Secretary of State is satisfied that any other relevant authority has failed to perform any functions which it ought to have performed, he may make an order declaring the authority to be in default.

(2) An order made by virtue of the preceding subsection which declares an authority to be in default may, for the purpose of remedying the default, direct the authority (hereafter in this section referred to as "the defaulting authority") to perform such of its functions as are specified in the order and may specify the manner in which and the time or times within which those functions are to be performed by the authority.

(3) If the defaulting authority fails to comply with any direction contained in such an order the Secretary of State may, instead of enforcing the order by mandamus, make an order transferring to himself such of the functions of the authority as he thinks fit.

(4) Where any functions of the defaulting authority are transferred in pursuance of the preceding subsection, the amount of any expenses which the Secretary of State certifies were incurred by him in performing those functions shall on demand be paid to him by the defaulting authority.

(5) Any expenses which in pursuance of the preceding subsection are required to be paid by the defaulting authority in respect of any functions transferred in pursuance of this section shall be defrayed by the authority in the like manner, and shall be debited to the like account, as if the functions had not been transferred and the expenses had been incurred by the authority in performing them; and the authority shall have the like powers for the purpose of raising any money required in pursuance of this subsection as the authority would have had for the purpose of raising money required for defraying expenses incurred for the purposes of the functions in question.

(6) An order transferring any functions of the defaulting authority in pursuance of subsection (3) of this section may provide for the transfer to the Secretary of State of such of the property, rights, liabilities and obligations of the authority as he considers appropriate; and where such an order is revoked the Secretary of State may, by the revoking order or a subsequent order, make such provision as he considers appropriate with respect to any property, rights, liabilities and obligations held by him for the purposes of the transferred functions.

(7) The Secretary of State may by order vary or revoke any order previously made by him in pursuance of this section.

(8) In this section "functions", in relation to an authority, means functions conferred on the authority by virtue of this Act.

(9) This section shall not apply to Scotland. [**132**]

DEFINITIONS

Functions:	sub-s. (8) and s. 98
Relevant authority:	s. 98

GENERAL NOTE

This again is a common form section to be found in several administrative statutes. However, in view of the many sections imposing duties on water and local authorities, this power may prove in practice to be of greater significance in this instance than has been the case with other default powers. No express provision is included enabling a "person aggrieved" by the failure of a "relevant authority" to perform some duty imposed by this Act, to complain to the Secretary of State (as is the case under s. 322 of the Public Health Act 1936), and therefore it would seem that an action for damages in respect of such a failure might lie at the suit of such a person, as the principle in *Pasmore* v *Oswaldtwistle Urban Council* [1898] A.C. 387 would not be relevant. Nevertheless, an informal complaint from a member of the public should be considered by the Secretary of State in view of his powers under this section. Without prejudice to the generality of the power conferred by this section, the Secretary of State is given a specific default power to revoke or modify a consent to a discharge under Part II, by virtue of section 37 (2).

SUB-S. (1)

Such an order should be made by statutory instrument: s. 104 (1).

SUB-S. (4)

If the expenses so chargeable to the relevant authority can be shown to be greater than the expenses that would have been incurred if the authority had carried out their duty, the district auditor may be able to take action by way of disallowance and reference to the court under Part VIII of the Local Government Act 1972.

98. Interpretation of Part V

In this Part of this Act—

"functions" includes powers and duties; and

"relevant authority" means—

(*a*) in England and Wales, the Secretary of State, a water authority, a county council, the Greater London Council, a district council, a London borough council, the Common Council of the City of London, the Sub-Treasurer of the Inner Temple and the Under Treasurer of the Middle Temple; and

(*b*) [*Applies to Scotland only.*] **[133]**

PART VI

MISCELLANEOUS AND GENERAL

Miscellaneous

99. Alteration of penalties

The enactments mentioned in Schedule 2 to this Act shall have effect subject to the provisions of that Schedule (which alter the penalties for the offences to which those enactments relate). **[134]**

100. Power to prohibit or restrict the importation and use, etc., of injurious substances

(1) The Secretary of State may by regulations prohibit or restrict—

(*a*) the importation into and the landing and unloading in the United Kingdom; or

(*b*) the use in connection with any trade or business or manufacturing process; or

(*c*) the supply for any purpose,

of any substance specified in the regulations (whether natural or artificial and whether in a solid or liquid or other form) if he considers it appropriate to do so for the purpose of preventing the substance from causing damage to persons, animals or plants or pollution of air, water or land.

(2) It shall be the duty of the Secretary of State before he makes any regulations in pursuance of the preceding subsection—

(*a*) to consult persons appearing to him to represent persons whose activities are likely to be prohibited or restricted by the proposed regulations; and

(*b*) to publish in the London Gazette, and in any other publication which he considers appropriate, a notice indicating the effect of the proposed regulations and specifying—

(i) the date on which it is proposed that the regulations should come into force, and

(ii) a place where a draft of the proposed regulations may be inspected free of charge by members of the public during office hours, and

(iii) a period of not less than fourteen days, beginning with the date on which the notice is first published, during which representations in writing may be made to the Secretary of State about the proposed regulations; and (*c*) to consider any representations which are made to him in accordance with the notice.

(3) [*Applies to Scotland only.*]

(4) The Secretary of State may, after performing the duty imposed on him by subsection (2) of this section with respect to any proposed regulations, make the regulations either—

(*a*) in the form of the draft mentioned in subsection (2) (*b*) (ii) of this section; or

(*b*) in that form with such modifications as he considers appropriate;

but the Secretary of State shall not make any regulations by virtue of paragraph (*b*) of this subsection unless he is of opinion that it is appropriate for the requirements of subsection (2) of this section to be disregarded in relation to the regulations.

(5) Regulations made in pursuance of this section may provide that a person who contravenes a specified provision of the regulations shall be guilty of an offence and may prescribe the maximum penalty for the offence (which shall not exceed, on summary conviction, a fine of £400 and, on conviction on indictment, imprisonment for a term of two years and a fine); but no proceedings for an offence against the regulations shall be brought in England and Wales except by or with the consent of the Director of Public Prosecutions. [**135**]

DEFINITION

Regulations: s. 105 (1), and see s. 104.

SUB-S. (1)

Contravention of such regulations will amount to an offence: sub-s. (5).

SUB-S. (2)

As to consultation, see note to s. 2 (2).

101. Disposal of waste, etc., by Atomic Energy Authority

Without prejudice to the powers of the United Kingdom Atomic Energy Authority apart from this section, the Authority shall have power—

(*a*) to engage in the United Kingdom and elsewhere in such activities relating to the treatment or disposal of waste and other matter as the Secretary of State may from time to time specify by notice given to the Authority; and

(*b*) to do anything which appears to the Authority to be appropriate for the purpose of exercising the powers conferred on the Authority by the preceding paragraph. [**136**]

PARA. (*a*)

"Waste" is not defined generally for the purposes of this Act, but see s. 30 (1) thereof (relevant only to Part I), and s. 19 (1) of the Radioactive Substances Act 1960.

102. Power to give effect to international agreements

(1) Regulations may provide that any provision of this Act, except this section, shall have effect with such modifications as are prescribed with a view to enabling the Government of the United Kingdom to give effect to any provision made by or under any international agreement to which the Government is for the time being a party.

(2) The Secretary of State may make, to the Commission established by the

Convention for the Prevention of Marine Pollution from Land-based Sources which was signed at Paris on behalf of the Government of the United Kingdom on 4th June 1974, such payments towards the expenses of the Commission as he may with the approval of the Treasury determine. [**137**]

DEFINITION

Regulations: made by the Secretary of State: s. 105 (1).

103. Adaptation of enactments to metric units

(1) The Secretary of State may by regulations amend—

(*a*) any provision of the Alkali Act or the Clean Air Acts 1956 and 1968; or

(*b*) any provision of an instrument made or having effect under any of those Acts,

by substituting an amount expressed in metric units for an amount not so expressed.

(2) Any amendments made in pursuance of the preceding subsection shall be such as to preserve the effect of the provisions mentioned in that subsection except to such extent as in the opinion of the Secretary of State is necessary to obtain amounts expressed in convenient and suitable terms. [**138**]

DEFINITION

Alkali Act: s. 105 (1)

General

104. Orders and regulations

(1) Any power conferred by this Act (except sections 59, 63 and 65 (6) to make an order or regulations—

(*a*) includes power to make different provision by the order or regulations for different circumstances and to include in the order or regulations such incidental, supplemental and transitional provisions as the person making the order or regulations considers appropriate in connection with the order or regulations; and

(*b*) shall be exercisable by statutory instrument except in the case of the powers conferred by section 97 of this Act;

and any statutory instrument made by virtue of this subsection, except an instrument containing only regulations made by virtue of section 18 of this Act or an order made by virtue of section 33 (4), 44 (5), 52, 53 or 109 (2) of this Act, shall be subject to annulment in pursuance of a resolution of either House of Parliament.

(2) No regulations shall be made by virtue of section 18 of this Act and no order shall be made by virtue of section 52 or 53 of this Act unless a draft of the regulations or order has been approved by a resolution of each House of Parliament.

(3) It shall be the duty of the Secretary of State, before he makes any regulations in pursuance of section 31 (5) of this Act—

(*a*) to publish in the London Gazette and in at least one newspaper circulating in the area in question a copy of the proposed regulations and a notice specifying—

(i) a period of not less than twenty-eight days, beginning with the date on which the notice is first published, within which objections to the proposed regulations may be made, and

(ii) the person to whom such objections may be made; and

(*b*) to consider any objections to the proposed regulations which are made within that period and, if such an objection is so made by a prescribed person and is not withdrawn, to cause a local inquiry to be held in pursuance of section 96 of this Act with respect to the proposed regulations;

and the Secretary of State may, after considering any such objections as are mentioned in paragraph (*b*) of this subsection and the report of any person appointed to hold a local inquiry with respect to the proposed regulations, make the regulations either in the form in which a copy of them was published in pursuance of this subsection or in that form with such modifications as he considers appropriate. [**139**]

GENERAL NOTE

This section was brought into force on 12th December 1974 by The Control of Pollution Act 1974 (Commencement No. 1) Order 1974 (S.I. 1974 No. 2039).

SUB-S. (1)

Sections 59 and 65 (6) refer to orders of a magistrates' court, and s. 63 refers to noise abatement orders, made by a local authority. Regulations and all other orders must be made by statutory instrument, as provided under the Statutory Instruments Act 1946. Regulations made under s. 18 or orders made under ss. 23 (4), 44 (5), 52, 53, or 109 (2), will not be subject to supervision in Parliament.

SUB-S. (3)

Local inquiry: see s. 96.

105. Interpretation etc.—general

(1) In this Act—

"the Alkali Act" means the Alkali, &c. Works Regulation Act 1906;

"county" and "district", except in relation to Scotland, have the same meanings as in the Local Government Act 1972;

"mine" and "quarry" have the same meanings as in the Mines and Quarries Act 1954;

"modifications" includes additions, omissions and amendments and "modify" and cognate expressions shall be construed accordingly;

"notice" means notice in writing;

"owner", except in relation to Scotland, means the person for the time being receiving the rackrent of the premises in connection with which the word is used, whether on his own account or as agent or trustee for another person, or who would so receive the rackrent if the premises were let at a rackrent;

"premises" includes land;

"prescribed" means prescribed by regulations;

"regulations" means regulations made by the Secretary of State;

"trade effluent" includes any liquid (either with or without particles of matter in suspension in it) which is discharged from premises used for carrying on any trade or industry, other than surface water and domestic sewerage, and for the purposes of this definition any premises wholly or mainly used (whether for profit or not) for agricultural or horticultural purposes or for scientific research or experiment shall be deemed to be premises used for carrying on a trade; and

"vessel" includes a hovercraft within the meaning of the Hovercraft Act 1968.

(2) Except so far as this Act expressly provides otherwise and subject to the provisions of section 33 of the Interpretation Act 1889 (which relates to offences under two or more laws), nothing in this Act—

(*a*) confers a right of action in any civil proceedings (other than proceedings for the recovery of a fine) in respect of any contravention of this Act or an instrument made in pursuance of this Act;

(*b*) affects any restriction imposed by or under any other enactment, whether public, local or private; or

(*c*) derogates from any right of action or other remedy (whether civil or criminal) in proceedings instituted otherwise than under this Act.

(3) In so far as any interest in Crown land is not an interest belonging to Her Majesty or a Crown interest or a Duchy interest, this Act shall apply to the land as if it were not Crown land; and expressions used in this subsection and subsection (7) of section 266 of the Town and Country Planning Act 1971 or, in relation to Scotland, subsection (7) of section 253 of the Town and Country Planning (Scotland) Act 1972 have the same meanings in this subsection as in that subsection.

(4) References in this Act to any enactment are references to it as amended by or under any other enactment. [**140**]

GENERAL NOTE

This section was brought into force on 12th December 1974 by The Control of Pollution Act 1974 (Commencement No. 1) Order 1974 (S.I. 1974 No. 2039).

SUB-S. (2)

As to civil proceedings arising out of matters that may amount to an offence under the Act, see s. 88.

SUB-S. (3)

Section 266 (7) of the Town and Country Planning Act 1971 provides that, for the purposes of that Act, "Crown land" means land in which there is a "Crown interest" or a "Duchy interest"; a "Crown interest" means an interest belonging to Her Majesty in right of the Crown, or belonging to a Government department, or held in trust for Her Majesty for the purposes of a Government department, and "Duchy interest" means an interest belonging to Her Majesty in right of the Duchy of Lancaster, or belonging to the Duchy of Cornwall.

106. [*Applies to Scotland only.*]

107. Application to Isles of Scilly

This Act shall have effect in its application to the Isles of Scilly with such modifications as the Secretary of State may by order specify, and the Secretary of State may by order vary or revoke any order previously made in pursuance of of this section. [**141**]

DEFINITION

As to orders, see s. 104

GENERAL NOTE

This section was brought into force on 12th December 1974 by The Control of Pollution Act 1974 (Commencement No. 1) Order 1974 (S.I. 1974 No. 2039).

108. Minor and consequential amendments of enactments, and repeals

(1) The enactments specified in Schedule 3 to this Act shall have effect subject to the amendments there specified (which are minor amendments and amendments consequential on provisions of this Act).

(2) The enactments mentioned in the first and second columns of Schedule 4 to this Act are hereby repealed to the extent specified in the third column of that Schedule.

(3) The Secretary of State may by order repeal or amend any provision of any local Act passed before this Act (including an Act confirming a provisional order) or of any order or other instrument made under an Act so passed if it appears to him that the provision is inconsistent with, or has become unnecessary or requires alteration in consequence of, any provision of this Act or corresponds to any provision repealed by this Act or relates to trade effluent. [**142**]

DEFINITION

As to orders, see s. 104

SUB-S. (1)

This subsection was brought into force on 12th December 1974 by The Control of Pollution Act 1974 (Commencement No. 1) Order 1974 (S.I. 1974 No. 2039), so far as it applies to para. 27 of Sch. 3.

109. Short title, commencement and extent

(1) This Act may be cited as the Control of Pollution Act 1974

(2) This Act shall come into force on such day as the Secretary of State may by order appoint; and—

(*a*) without prejudice to the generality of section 104 (1) (*a*) of this Act, different days may be appointed in pursuance of this subsection for different provisions of this Act and for such different purposes of the same provision as may be specified in the order;

(*b*) any provision appointing a day in pursuance of this subsection may be revoked or varied by an order made by the Secretary of State which comes into force before that day.

(3) This Act, except sections 75, 77, 100 and 101 and this section, does not extend to Northern Ireland. [**143**]

SUB-S. (2)

An order made under this subsection must be made by statutory instrument, but it will not be subject to the negative resolution procedure: s. 104 (1).

At the date of going to press the following Commencement order had been made: The Control of Pollution Act 1974 (Commencement No. 1) Order 1974 (J.I. 1974 No. 2009).

SCHEDULES

SCHEDULE 1

Section 63 (4)

NOISE ABATEMENT ZONES

1. A local authority shall after making any noise abatement order—

(*a*) serve on every owner, lessee and occupier (other than tenants for a month or any period less than a month) of any of the premises within the area to which the order relates; and

(*b*) publish in the London Gazette and once at least in each of two successive weeks in some newspaper circulating in the area to which the order relates,

a notice complying with the requirements set out in the following paragraph. [**144**]

2. The requirements referred to in the preceding paragraph are that the notice shall—

(*a*) state that the order has been made, and its general effect;

(*b*) specify a place in the area of the local authority where a copy of the order and of any map or plan referred to therein may be inspected by any person free of charge at all reasonable times during a period of not less than six weeks from the date of the notice; and

(*c*) state that within the said period any person who will be affected by the order may by notice to the Secretary of State object to the confirmation of the order. **[145]**

3.—(1) If no objection is duly made to the Secretary of State within the said period, or if every objection so made is withdrawn, the Secretary of State may, if he thinks fit, confirm the order with or without modifications.

(2) In any other case he shall, subject of the following provisions of this paragraph, before confirming the order—

(*a*) cause a local inquiry to be held in pursuance of section 96 of this Act; or

(*b*) afford to any person by whom an objection has been duly made as aforesaid and not withdrawn an opportunity of appearing before and being heard by a person appointed by him for the purpose;

and, after considering the objection and the report of the person who held the inquiry or the person appointed as aforesaid, he may confirm the order with or without modifications.

(3) The Secretary of State may confirm the order (with or without modifications) without complying with the preceding sub-paragraph if he is satisfied that compliance is unnecessary having regard to—

(*a*) the nature of the premises to which the order will relate when it comes into force; or

(*b*) the nature of the interests of the persons who have made objections which have not been withdrawn.

(4) Where the order varies or revokes a previous order, the Secretary of State may, in acting under sub-paragraph (2) above, disregard any objection to the order which in his opinion amounts in substance to an objection which was made to the previous order. **[146]**

4. An order when confirmed shall come into operation on such date as may be specified in the order which, except in the case of an order revoking an existing order or varying an existing order by excluding from it any specified class of premises, shall not be a date earlier than one month from the date of confirmation:

Provided that if, before the date on which the order is to come into operation, the local authority—

(*a*) passes a resolution postponing the coming into operation of the order; and

(*b*) publishes a notice stating the effect of the resolution in the London Gazette and once at least in each of two successive weeks in a newspaper circulating in the area to which the order relates,

the order shall, unless there is a further postponement under paragraph (*a*) of this proviso, come into operation on the date specified in the resolution. **[147]**

5. A local authority shall not exercise its powers under the proviso to the preceding paragraph to postpone the coming into operation of a noise abatement order for a period of, or for periods amounting in all to, more than twelve months without the consent of the Secretary of State. **[148]**

DEFINITIONS

Local authority:	s. 73
Noise abatement order:	s. 63 (5)
Owner:	s. 105 (1)
Premises:	s. 105 (1)

PARA. 1

Service of such notices should be effected in accordance with s. 233 of the Local Government Act 1972.

PARA. 4

Postponement resolution: see para. 5.

SCHEDULE 2

Section 99

Alteration of Penalties

1–3. [*Apply to Scotland only.*]

The Alkali, &c., Works Regulation Act 1906

4. In section 12 (4) of the Alkali Act (under which obstruction of an inspector is punishable on summary conviction by a fine not exceeding £10) for the words "ten pounds" there shall be substituted the word "£100". **[149]**

5. In section 16A of that Act (which provides for certain offences under other provisions of that Act to be punishable on summary conviction by a fine not exceeding £100 or £20 a day in the case of certain continuing offences) for the words "one hundred pounds" in both places where they occur there shall be substituted the word "£400" and for the words "twenty pounds" there shall be substituted the word "£50". **[150]**

The Public Health Act 1936

6. In section 19 (3) of the Public Health Act 1936 (under which a person is liable on summary conviction to a fine not exceeding £50 if he constructs a drain or sewer in a manner other than that in which he is required to construct it by a local authority in pursuance of that section) for the words "fifty pounds" there shall be substituted the word "£200". **[151]**

7. In section 27 of that Act (which provides that certain matters are not to be passed into public sewers), in subsection (2) (under which a contravention of that section is punishable on summary conviction by a fine not exceeding £10 and a further £5 for each day on which the offence continues after conviction) for the words from "to a fine" onwards there shall be substituted the words—

"(*a*) on summary conviction, to a fine not exceeding £400 and to a further fine not exceeding £50 for each day on which the offence continues after conviction therefor;

(*b*) on conviction on indictment, to imprisonment for a term not exceeding two years or a fine or both".

8. In section 34 (5) of that Act (under which a person who causes a drain or sewer to connect with a public sewer in contravention of that section is liable on summary conviction to a fine not exceeding £20) for the words "twenty pounds" there shall be substituted the word "£200". **[152]**

9. In section 36 (1) of that Act (under which a person who causes a drain or sewer to communicate with a pubic sewer after the local authority have given notice that they intend themselves to make the connection is liable on summary conviction to a fine not exceeding £50) for the words "fifty pounds" there shall be substituted the word "£200". **[153]**

10. In section 41 (3) of that Act (under which a person is liable on summary conviction to a fine not exceeding £5 if he does certain work in connection with an underground drain which communicates with a sewer without giving 24 hours notice to the relevant local authority of his intention to do so or if he does not permit an authorised officer of the local authority free access to the work) for the words "five pounds" there shall be substituted the word "£100". **[154]**

11. In section 94 (2) of that Act (under which a person who fails to abate a nuisance or to take adequate steps to prevent a recurrence of a nuisance is liable on summary conviction to a fine not exceeding £20) for the word "£20" there shall be substituted the word "£200". **[155]**

12. In section 95 (1) of that Act (under which a person who contravenes or fails to comply with a nuisance order is liable on summary conviction to a fine not

exceeding £50 and a further £5 for each day on which the offence continues after conviction) for the words "£50" and "£5" there shall be substituted the words "£400" and "£50" respectively. **[156]**

The Public Health (Drainage of Trade Premises) Act 1937

13. In section 2 of the Public Health (Drainage of Trade Premises) Act 1937 (under which restrictions are imposed on the discharge of trade effluent), in subsection (5) (under which an occupier of premises is guilty of an offence if trade effluent is discharged in contravention of the section or without any consent necessary for the purposes of the Act or if any direction or condition given or imposed under that section is contravened) after the words "guilty" of an offence there shall be inserted the words "and liable on summary conviction to a fine not exceeding £200 and to a further fine not exceeding £50 for every day on which the offence continues after conviction therefor." **[157]**

14. In section 9 of that Act (under which a person who fails to give specified information to a water authority is liable on summary conviction to a fine not exceeding £5 and a further £2 for each day on which the offence continues after conviction) for the words "five pounds" and "forty shillings" there shall be substituted the words "£50" and "£5" respectively. **[158]**

The Water Act 1945

15. In section 19 (3) of the Water Act 1945 (under which byelaws made under section 17 of that Act or section 22 (6) of the Countryside Act 1968 may contain provision making any person who contravenes the byelaws liable to a fine not exceeding £20 and a further £5 for each day during which the offence continues after conviction) for the words "twenty pounds" and "five pounds" there shall be substituted the words "£400" and "£50" respectively. **[159]**

16. In section 21 of that Act (under which a person is guilty of an offence if he is guilty of any act or neglect whereby any spring, well, borehole or adit the water from which is used or likely to be used for human consumption or domestic purposes or for manufacturing food or drink for human consumption is polluted or likely to be polluted) after subsection (2) there shall be inserted the following subsection—

"(3) Any person guilty of an offence by virtue of this section shall be liable in respect of each offence—

(*a*) on summary conviction, to a fine not exceeding £400 and in the case of a continuing offence to a further fine not exceeding £50 for every day during which the offence is continued after conviction;

(*b*) on conviction on indictment, to a fine or to imprisonment for a term not exceeding two years or to both a fine and such imprisonment."

17, 18. [*Apply to Scotland only.*] **[160]**

The Clean Air Act 1956

19.—(1) In subsection (1) of section 27 of the Clean Air Act 1956 (under which a person is on summary conviction liable in respect of an emission of dark smoke from a building to a fine not exceeding £20 in the case of an emission from a private dwelling and not exceeding £100 in the case of other emissions) for the word "£20" there shall be substituted the word "£100" and for the words "one hundred pounds" there shall be substituted the words "£400 or, in the case of an offence under that section as applied to vessels by section 20 of this Act, £1,000".

(2) In subsection (2) of that section (under which a person who fails to notify the local authority of the installation of a furnace or who occupies a building in a smoke control area from which smoke is emitted is liable on summary conviction to a fine not exceeding £20) for the word "£20" there shall be substituted the word "£100".

(3) In subsection (3) of that section (under which a person who unlawfully discloses information furnished or obtained under that Act is liable on summary conviction to a fine not exceeding £100 and to imprisonment for a term not exceeding three months) for the words from "one hundred pounds" onwards there shall be substituted the word "£400".

(4) In subsection (4) of that section (under which a person who is guilty of any other offence under that Act is liable on summary conviction to a fine not exceeding £100) for the words "one hundred pounds" in both places where they occur there shall be substituted the word "£400" and for the words "twenty pounds" there shall be substituted the word "£50". **[161]**

The Radioactive Substances Act 1960

20.—(1) In subsection (2) of section 13 of the Radioactive Substances Act 1960 (which provides among other things that a person who keeps radioactive material or mobile radioactive apparatus or who disposes of or accumulates radioactive waste contrary to the provisions of the Act shall be liable on summary conviction to a fine not exceeding £100 and to imprisonment for a term not exceeding three months) for the words "one hundred pounds" there shall be substituted the word "£400".

(2) In subsection (4) of that section (under which a person who unlawfully discloses information furnished or obtained under that Act is liable on summary conviction to a fine not exceeding £50 and to imprisonment for a term not exceeding three months) for the words "fifty pounds" there shall be substituted the word "£400".

(3) In subsection (5) of that section (under which a person who fails to exhibit a certificate of registration or an authorisation or who obstructs an inspector or fails to provide information is liable on summary conviction to a fine not exceeding £50 and to imprisonment for a term not exceeding three months) for the words from "fifty pounds" onwards there shall be substituted the words "£100 and on conviction on indictment to a fine".

(4) In subsection (6) of that section (under which a person who pulls down or defaces a certificate or authorisation is liable on summary conviction to a fine not exceeding £10) for the words "ten pounds" there shall be substituted the word "£20". **[162]**

21–25. [*Apply to Scotland only.*]

The Clean Air Act 1968

26. In the following provisions of the Clean Air Act 1968 (which provide that a person who commits an offence mentioned in any of those provisions is liable on summary conviction to a fine not exceeding £100), namely—

(*a*) section 1 (1) (which prohibits the emission of dark smoke from any industrial or trade premises);

(*b*) section 2 (2) (which penalises the emission of grit or dust, from a chimney serving a furnace to which the section applies, at a rate exceeding a prescribed limit);

(*c*) section 2 (4) (which penalises a failure to use any practicable means of minimising the emission of grit or dust from a chimney for which no limit is prescribed);

(*d*) section 3 (3) (which penalises the use of certain furnaces which are not fitted with appropriate plant for arresting grit and dust);

(*e*) section 4 (7) (which penalises the use for certain purposes of furnaces which are exempt from the operation of section 3 (1) of that Act); and

(*f*) section 6 (1) and (2) (which penalise the use of certain furnaces unless they are served by chimneys of approved heights and any conditions of the approvals are complied with),

for the word "£100" there shall be substituted the word "£400". **[163]**

27. In section 9 (1) of that Act (under which a person who acquires or sells by retail any unauthorised solid fuel for use in a smoke control area is liable on summary conviction to a fine not exceeding £20) for the word "£20" there shall be substituted the word "£100". [**164**]

SCHEDULE 3

Section 108

MINOR AND CONSEQUENTIAL AMENDMENTS OF ENACTMENTS

The Alkali, &c. Works Regulation Act 1906

1. Sections 3, 4 and 5 of the Alkali Act (alkali waste), section 14 (appointment of additional inspectors) and section 15 (power of owners of works to make special rules) shall cease to have effect. [**165**]

2. Section 8 of that Act (which is superseded by paragraph 4 of this Schedule) shall cease to have effect. [**166**]

3.—(1) In section 27 of that Act as amended by the Alkali, &c. Works Order 1966, in the definition of "noxious or offensive gas" the words "except that arising solely from the combustion of coal", in both places where they occur, shall be omitted and for the words "Sulphurous anhydride" there shall be substituted the words "Sulphur dioxide".

(2) The amendments made by the preceding sub-paragraph may be varied or revoked as if they were contained in the said Order of 1966. [**167**]

4.—(1) At the end of Schedule 1 to that Act, as amended by the Alkali, &c. Works Order 1966 and the Alkali, &c. Works Order 1971 and in Scotland by the Alkali, &c., Works (Scotland) Order 1972, there shall be added the following paragraph—

"(61) Smelting works, that is to say works in which sulphide ores are calcinated or smelted."

(2) The said paragraph (61) may be varied or revoked as if it were contained in the said Orders of 1971 and 1972. [**168**]

The Salmon and Freshwater Fisheries Act 1923

5. In section 9 (5) of the Salmon and Freshwater Fisheries Act 1923 (which provides that certain activities authorised by that section shall not constitute an offence under provisions which include section 2 (1) (*a*) of the Rivers (Prevention of Pollution) Act 1951) for the words "section 2 (1) (*a*) of the Rivers (Prevention of Pollution) Act 1951" there shall be substituted the words "and section 31 (1) (*a*) of the Control of Pollution Act 1974". [**169**]

The Public Health Act 1936

6. In section 3 (1) (*b*) of the Public Health Act 1936 (under which an order constituting a port health authority may, among other things, assign to the authority any functions conferred on a local authority by that Act) after the words "this Act" there shall be inserted the words "or the Control of Pollution Act 1974". [**170**]

7. Sections 79 and 80 of that Act (which relate to the removal of noxious matter, manure and refuse from premises) shall cease to have effect. [**171**]

The Public Health (Drainage of Trade Premises) Act 1937

8. Sections 2 (4) and 3 (2) of the Public Health (Drainage of Trade Premises) Act 1937 and the proviso in section 7 (1) of that Act (which relate to the protection of interested bodies within the meaning of that Act) shall cease to have effect. [**172**]

9. In section 4 (5) of that Act (under which disputes arising under that Act as to the discharges of trade effluent which were made during such a period as is mentioned in subsections (1) or (2) of that section are to be determined by the Secretary of State) for the words "this Act" there shall be substituted the words "section 43 of the Control of Pollution Act 1974" and for the words "is mentioned" there shall be substituted the words "before the repeal of those subsections by that Act was mentioned". [**173**]

10. In section 10 (1) of that Act (which authorises the taking of samples of trade effluent which is passing from premises into a public sewer) after the word "passing" there shall be inserted the words ", either directly or through a private drain or sewer,". [**174**]

11–15. [*Apply to Scotland only.*]

The Clean Air Act 1956

16. (1) In subsection (1) of section 30 of the Clean Air Act 1956 (early notification to be confirmed in writing within 48 hours of becoming aware of the offence) for the words "within forty-eight hours after" there shall be substituted the words "before the end of the four days next following the day on which".

(2) In subsection (2) of that section (presumption in favour of defendant if notification not given within two days after the day of the offence) for the words "two days" there shall be substituted the words "four days".

(3) This paragraph shall not apply where the offence was committed before the coming into force of this paragraph. [**175**]

The Rivers (Prevention of Pollution) Act 1961

17. In section 10 (1) of the Rivers (Prevention of Pollution) Act 1961 (which among other things relates to inspection chambers provided in compliance with conditions imposed under that Act) and in section 12 (1) (ii) of that Act (which authorises the disclosure in connection with the execution of that Act of information of which the disclosure is restricted by that section) the reference to that Act shall include a reference to this Act. [**176**]

The Public Health Act 1961

18. At the end of section 34 (5) of the Public Health Act 1961 (which among other things provides that "rubbish" in that section does not include material accumulated in the course of business) there shall be inserted the words "or waste deposited in accordance with a disposal licence in force under Part I of the Control of Pollution Act 1974". [**177**]

The London Government Act 1963

19. In section 41 (1) (*b*) of the London Government Act 1963 (which enables the functions, rights and liabilities of a local authority under any of the provisions there mentioned to be assigned to the port health authority for the Port of London) after the words "section 87 of this Act" there shall be inserted the words "and under any provision of the Control of Pollution Act 1974". [**178**]

The Water Resources Act 1963

20. In section 77 (2) of the Water Resources Act 1963 (which refers to sewage effluent within the meaning of the Rivers (Prevention of Pollution) Act 1951) for the words "the Rivers (Prevention of Pollution) Act 1951" there shall be substituted the words "Part II of the Control of Pollution Act 1974". [**179**]

21. In section 113 (1) of that Act (which authorises water authorities to take samples of certain effluents) for the words "Clean Rivers (Estuaries and Tidal Waters) Act 1960" in paragraph (*c*) there shall be substituted the words "Part II of the Control of Pollution Act 1974". **[180]**

The Housing Act 1964

22. In section 95 of the Housing Act 1964 after subsection (2) (power of local authority to resolve to exclude heating appliances from eligibility for grant) there shall be inserted the following subsection—

"(2A) The Secretary of State may, when confirming the order to which a resolution under subsection (2) above relates, direct that the resolution shall have effect subject to such modifications as may be specified in the direction, or may direct that the resolution shall not have effect." **[181]**

23, 24. [*Apply to Scotland only.*]

The Civic Amenities Act 1967

25.—(1) In section 18 (1) of the Civic Amenities Act 1967 (which requires local authorities to provide places where certain refuse can be deposited at all reasonable times free of charge by persons resident in the authorities' areas and on payment by other persons) after the word "times" there shall be inserted the words "(including at least one period of time on the Saturday or the following day of each week except a week in which the Saturday is 25th December or 1st January)", and for the words from "persons resident" onwards there shall be substituted the words "any person".

(2) In section 23 of that Act, for subsection (3) (by which section 76 of the Public Health Act 1936, which is repealed by this Act, is applied for the purposes of that section) there shall be substituted the following subsection—

"(3) A local authority may—

(*a*) provide places for the deposit of any thing removed by them under subsection (1) of this section;

(*b*) provide plant and apparatus for the treatment or disposal of any thing deposited at such a place; and

(*c*) sell or otherwise dispose of any such thing." **[182]**

The Hovercraft Act 1968

26. In section 1 (1) (*g*) of the Hovercraft Act 1968 for the words "no proceedings in pursuance of the Noise Abatement Act 1960" there shall be substituted the words "no proceedings in pursuance of Part III of the Control of Pollution Act 1974". **[183]**

The Water Act 1973

27. For the purposes of section 14 of the Water Act 1973 (under which, among other things, functions of local authorities with respect to sewerage and sewage disposal, including certain functions under Part XII of the Public Health Act 1936, were transferred to water authorities), section 306 of the said Act of 1936 (which related to the compulsory purchase of land and was contained in the said Part XII) shall have effect from 31st March 1974 as if that section had not been repealed by the Local Government Act 1972. **[184]**

28. In subsection (12) of section 24 of that Act (which relates to reports of surveys prepared by water authorities under that section) after paragraph (*a*) there shall be inserted the following paragraph—

"(*aa*) shall secure that a copy of each such report and of all such amendments is available at the principal office of the authority for inspection by the public free of charge at all reasonable hours." **[185]**

29. In section 36 (3) of that Act (which among other things provides that Part II of Schedule 7 to that Act shall have effect with respect to the making of byelaws by water authorities under any enactment) the last reference to any enactment shall be construed as including a reference to any enactment passed after that Act. [**186**]

30. In paragraph 17 (2) of Schedule 7 to that Act (which relates to the confirmation of byelaws made by a water authority under section 5 of the Rivers (Prevention of Pollution) Act 1951) for the words "section 5 of the Rivers (Prevention of Pollution) Act 1951" there shall be substituted the words "section 31 (6) or 33 (1) of the Control of Pollution Act 1974" and after the words "a stream" there shall be inserted the words "or the controlled waters (within the meaning of Part II of that Act)". [**187**]

31. [*Applies to Scotland only.*]

GENERAL NOTE

Amendments worth noting include (4) adding another item to the list of "scheduled works"; (7) repealing ss. 79 and 80 of the Public Health Act 1936 (not often used in practice); (10) enabling samples of trade effluent to be taken from a private drain or sewer, when the effluent is passing through into a public sewer; (12) providing for a longer time limit for the "intimation" notice (as it is sometimes called) before proceedings are commenced under the Clean Air Act 1956; (25) as to opening hours for public refuse tips which are in future to be made available to all persons (free of charge), and not only to residents; (27) which restores s. 306 of the Public Health Act 1936 for the benefit of water authorities when pursuing their functions under s. 14 of the Water Act 1974, and (29) and (30), relating to the making of byelaws by water authorities.

SCHEDULE 4

Section 108

Repeals

Chapter	Short Title	Extent of Repeal
25 & 26 Vict. c. 97	The Salmon Fisheries (Scotland) Act 1862	Section 13.
38 & 39 Vict. c. 55	The Public Health Act 1875	Section 148, but not so as to affect any agreement in force under that section.
55 & 56 Vict. c. 55	The Burgh Police (Scotland) Act 1892	Sections 107 to 109. In section 110, the words from "and may place" to "or nuisance." Sections 111 to 114. Section 116.
58 & 59 Vict. c. 42	The Sea Fisheries Regulation (Scotland) Act 1895	Section 8 (1) (*f*).
60 & 61 Vict. c. 38	The Public Health (Scotland) Act 1897	In section 39, the first paragraph.
3 Edw. 7 c. 33	The Burgh Police (Scotland) Act 1903	Section 23. In section 24, the words "the immediately preceding section or under".

Chapter	Short Title	Extent of Repeal
6 Edw. 7 c. 14	The Alkali, &c. Works Regulation Act 1906	Sections 3, 4, 5 and 8. In section 9 (1) the words "a cement work, or a smelting work". In section 11 (*b*) the words "or with the treatment of alkali waste". Section 12 (1) (*d*). Sections 14, 15 and 17. In section 18, in subsection (1) the words "other than an offence against a special rule" and subsection (4). Section 19. In section 20 the words "other than an offence against a special rule". In section 22 (1) the words from "or that any alkali waste is deposited" to "contravention of this Act". In section 28, in paragraph (*b*) the words "offences against special rules and" and paragraph (*c*).
13 & 14 Geo. 5 c. 16	The Salmon and Freshwater Fisheries Act 1923	In section 9 (5) the words from "and section 22 (1) (*a*)" onwards.
24 & 25 Geo. 5 c. 40	The Administration of Justice (Appeals) Act 1934	In the Schedule, the entry amending section 17 (5) of the Alkali Act.
26 Geo. 5 & 1 Edw. 8 c. 49	The Public Health Act 1936	Sections 72 to 77, 79, 80 and 259 (2).
1 Edw. 8 and 1 1 Geo. 6 c. 5	The Trunk Roads Act 1936	Section 6 (6).
1 Edw. 8 and 1 Geo. 6 c. 40	The Public Health (Drainage of Trade Premises) Act 1937	Section 2 (4), 3 (2) and 4 (1) to (3). In section 7 (1), the proviso. Section 11. In section 14 (1), the definition of "interested body".
8 & 9 Geo. 6 c. 42	The Water Act 1945	Section 18.
14 & 15 Geo. 6 c. 64	The Rivers (Prevention of Pollution) Act 1951	The whole Act.
14 & 15 Geo. 6 c. 66	The Rivers (Prevention of Pollution) (Scotland) Act 1951	The whole Act except sections 1, 6 (1), 7, 9, 10 (1), 12 (1) to (3) and (4) (*a*) and (*c*), 13, 16, 17, 18 (1) to (3), 19, 32 (1), in section 35 (1) the definitions of "contravention", "functions", "land", "local authority", "local water authority", "river purification authority", "river purification board", "stream" and

Chapter	Short Title	Extent of Repeal
14 & 15 Geo. 6 c. 66	The Rivers (Prevention of Pollution) (Scotland) Act 1951	"tidal waters", section 36 (1) and (5) and Schedule 4.
1 & 2 Eliz. 2 c. 26	The Local Government (Miscellaneous Provisions) Act 1953	Section 8.
4 & 5 Eliz. 2 c. 52	The Clean Air Act 1956	In section 16 (1) in the proviso, paragraph (i). In section 25, paragraphs (*a*) and (*b*). In section 26, the words "manufacturing process or". In Schedule 2, the amendments of sections 3, 8 and 18 of the Alkali Act.
7 & 8 Eliz. 2 c. 25	The Highways Act 1959	In section 228 (9) the words "section one hundred and forty-eight of the Public Health Act 1875".
8 & 9 Eliz. 2 c. 34	The Radioactive Substances Act 1960	In Schedule 1, in paragraph 3 the words "seventy-nine", in paragraph 6 the word "eighteen" and paragraphs 7, 8A and 15.
8 & 9 Eliz. 2 c. 54	The Clean Rivers (Estuaries & Tidal Waters) Act 1960	The whole Act.
8 & 9 Eliz. 2 c. 68	The Noise Abatement Act 1960	The whole Act, but not so as to affect notices served by virtue of section 1 of the Act before the coming into force of section 58 of this Act.
9 & 10 Eliz. 2 c. 50	The Rivers (Prevention of Pollution) Act 1961	The whole Act except sections 10, 12, 13 (1) and 15 (1) and (3).
1961 c. 64	The Public Health Act 1961	Sections 55 to 58 and 63 (5).
1963 c. 33	The London Government Act 1963	In section 40 (4) (*d*), the reference to section 8 of the Local Government (Miscellaneous Provisions) Act 1953, and section 40 (4) (*g*). In Part I of Schedule 11, paragraphs 14, 16 and 32.
1963 c. 38	The Water Resources Act 1963	Sections 72 to 76. In section 79, subsections (1), (2) and (7), in subsection (5) the words "by virtue of subsection (1) of this section or" and in subsection (8) the words from "(including" to "section)". In section 114, in subsection (1) the words from the first "or" to "section" and the words "or discharge", and subsections (2) and (4) (*a*). In section 115 (1) (*b*) the words from "or" to "thereof".

Chapter	Short Title	Extent of Repeal
1963 c. 38—*contd.*	The Water Resources Act 1963—*contd.*	In section 135 (8) the word "72". In Schedule 13, paragraphs 5, 6, 7, 11 and 14.
1965 c. 13	The Rivers (Prevention of Pollution) (Scotland) Act 1965	The whole Act except sections 10, 13 (1), 15 (1) and (4) and 17 (1) to (3).
1965 c. 36	The Gas Act 1965	Section 4 (5).
1966 c. 38	The Sea Fisheries Regulation Act 1966	Section 5 (1) (*c*).
1967 c. 69	The Civic Amenities Act 1967	Section 23 (6) (*a*).
1967 c. 80	The Criminal Justice Act 1967	In Schedule 3, the entry relating to section 114 of the Burgh Police (Scotland) Act 1892, in the entry relating to section 22 of the Public Health (Scotland) Act 1897 the words "(as extended by section 1 (5) of the Noise Abatement Act 1960)", and the entries relating to sections 76 (3), 94 (2) and 95 (1) (both as originally enacted and as applied by section 16 (1) of the Clean Air Act 1956) of the Public Health Act 1936 and section 27 (1) and (2) of the Clean Air Act 1956.
1968 c. 41	The Countryside Act 1968	Section 22 (6) (*c*) and (8).
1972 c. 21	The Deposit of Poisonous Waste Act 1972	The whole Act.
1972 c. 70	The Local Government Act 1972	Section 180 (3) (*d*) and (*g*). In section 236 (2) the words "or 18". In Schedule 14, in paragraph 4 the words "79, 80" and paragraphs 5 to 8 and 49.
1973 c. 37	The Water Act 1973	Section 17 (1) to (4). Paragraph 5 of Schedule 2. Paragraph 63 of Schedule 8.
1973 c. 65	The Local Government (Scotland) Act 1973	In section 135 (3), the words from "and the said areas" to the end. Section 136. In Schedule 16, paragraphs 7 to 9. In Schedule 28, paragraph 69.

[188]

GENERAL NOTE

The whole of the Rivers (Prevention of Pollution) Act 1951 is repealed, but a few sections of the 1961 Act of the same title are still alive. The whole of the

Deposit of Poisonous Waste Act 1972 disappears, and so do a few sections of the Public Health Acts 1936 and 1961. Notice also the considerable number of of repeals in the Alkali Act 1906. The Noise Abatement Act 1960 also is repealed. As to repeals of local Acts by order made by the Secretary of State, see s. 108 (3). The Clean Rivers (Estuaries and Tidal Waters) Act 1960 is repealed as being no longer of any effect.

INDEX

All references are to paragraph numbers

All references are to paragraph numbers

Index

All references are to paragraph numbers

All references are to paragraph numbers

All references are to paragraph numbers

All references are to paragraph numbers

All references are to paragraph numbers